a **WEE GUIDE** *to*
William Wallace

a **WEE GUIDE** *to*

William Wallace

Duncan Jones

GOBLINSHEAD

Edinburgh

a **WEE GUIDE** to William Wallace

First Published 1997
Reprinted 1998, 1999, 2001, 2002
© Martin Coventry 1997
Text © Duncan Jones & Martin Coventry 1997
Published by **GOBLINSHEAD**
130B Inveresk Road
Musselburgh EH21 7AY
Scotland
tel 0131 665 2894; *fax* 0131 653 6566
email goblinshead@sol.co.uk

British Library Cataloguing in Publication Data
A catalogue record for this book is available from the British Library.

ISBN 1 899874 08 9

Typeset by **GOBLINSHEAD** using Desktop Publishing
Typeset in Garamond Narrow

WEE GUIDES
William Wallace
The Picts
Scottish History
The Jacobites
Robert Burns
Mary, Queen of Scots
Robert the Bruce
Haunted Castles of Scotland
Old Churches and Abbeys of Scotland
Castles and Mansions of Scotland
New for 1999
Prehistoric Scotland
Macbeth and Early Scotland
Whisky

a **WEE GUIDE** *to*
William Wallace

Contents

List of maps and plans

List of illustrations

Acknowledgements

Many thanks to the following for their kind permission to use illustrations:

William Hole: Battle of Stirling Bridge, mural (cover) The Scottish National Portrait Gallery.

National Wallace Monument (page 29), sword of William Wallace (page 26), National Wallace Monument – aerial view (page 77) Argyll, the Isles, Loch Lomond, Stirling and Trossachs Tourist Board.

Coat of arms of William Wallace (pages 9 & 67), William Wallace (pages 17 & 82), Death of William Heselrig (page 21), Battle of Stirling Bridge (page 33), Wallace is knighted (page 42), and the Trial of Sir William Wallace (page 65) by Catriona Campbell.

Dunbar Castle (page 15), Roxburgh Castle (page 27), Dumbarton Castle (page 37) from collection of Grace Ellis.

Battle plans by Duncan Jones.

Maps and photographs by Martin Coventry.

Other illustrations from collection of Martin Coventry.

How to use this book

This book is divided into two sections:

- The text (pages 5–67) describes William Wallace's life and events surrounding him, with maps (pages 4, 18, 44). A calendar of events summarises the period chronologically (pages 2–3). Plans illustrate the battles at Stirling Bridge and Falkirk (pages 32, 34, 48, 49).

- Places, associated with William Wallace, to visit (pages 69–79) listing over 30 castles, abbeys and places in Scotland and England. Information includes access, opening, facilities, and a brief description; and a map locates all the sites in Scotland (page 68).

The Legacy of William Wallace looks at Wallace's life and times as patriot and man (pages 80–3).

An index (pages 84–5) lists all the main people, places, battles and events.

Introduction

William Wallace is one of the greatest, and most mysterious, characters from Scottish history. The second son of a minor landed family from Elderslie, near Paisley, he burst onto the historical scene in 1297 and rose to become, if only for a year, Guardian of the Community of the Realm of Scotland. Although he finally met defeat, and was brutally executed by the English King, Edward I, his actions in defence of his native land inspired his fellow countrymen to fight on and, at last, to win their freedom.

Numerous myths – both old and new – surround him, and make it very difficult to get a clear picture of the man and his times. I have tried here to give a concise account of Wallace's life, based as far as possible on firm evidence, and to put his deeds into a relevant historical context.

I am deeply grateful to everyone who has helped and encouraged me in writing this book. Special thanks go to Catriona Campbell, Martin Coventry, Joyce Miller, Grace Ellis, Patrick Parsons and Alison Rae.

DJ, Glasgow, April 1997

For Natalie

Calendar of events

1270–5? Birth of William Wallace.

1286   Death of Alexander III.
        Election of Guardians.

1289   Treaty of Salisbury.

1290   Treaty of Birgham. Death of Maid of Norway.

1291   Edward I accepted as superior lord of Scotland. Court of claims
        opened.

1292   Balliol crowned King of Scots.

1294   War between England and France. Welsh revolt.

1295   Council of Twelve replaces King John. Treaty between France
        and Scotland.

1296   War between England and Scotland. Sack of Berwick. Battle of
        Dunbar. King John abdicates. Edward I receives homage at
        Berwick Parliament (Ragman Roll).

1297   Wallace kills William Heselrig, Sheriff of Lanark, and forces
        William Ormesby, the English justiciar in Scotland, to flee. A
        general Scottish uprising begins under Andrew Murray and
        William Wallace. The nobles join in but capitulate at Irvine. Battle
        of Stirling Bridge. Wallace raids the northern English counties.
        William Lamberton appointed Bishop of St Andrews. Andrew
        Murray dies.

1298   Wallace knighted and appointed sole Guardian. Edward I invades
        Scotland. Battle of Falkirk. Wallace resigns Guardianship. Bruce
        and John Comyn appointed Guardians.

1299   Scots achieve diplomatic successes in France and Rome. Bishop
        Lamberton appointed third Guardian. Scots recapture Stirling
        Castle. Wallace travels to the Continent.

1300   Bruce resigns Guardianship, replaced by Ingram de Umfraville.
        Wallace travels Europe on diplomatic missions. English invasion
        of Scotland. Siege of Caerlaverock. Pressure from France and
        Papacy forces Edward to sign a truce.

1301   John Soulis appointed sole Guardian. English invasion.

1302   Balliol released into French custody. Edward forced to make a
        second truce. Bruce submits to Edward I. Wallace returns to
        Scotland.

1303   Wallace begins to lead attacks against English garrisons in Scotland. Battle of Roslin. Treaty between England and France, excluding Scots. Edward I invades Scotland for the last time.

1304   Wallace defeated at Happrew. Many Scots submit to Edward I. Stirling Castle falls to the English. Wallace becomes a fugitive.

1305   Betrayed by Menteith, Wallace is captured. He is taken to London where he is tried, convicted and brutally executed.

Map 1: 1286–96 (Chapters 1–2)

Ross

Elgin

Buchan

Strathbogie

•Inverness

Moray

Badenoch

Mar

Aberdeen•

SCOTLAND

Mearns

Atholl

◄•Montrose

Angus

Scone   •Dundee

Perth•

St Andrews

Fife

Argyll

Strathearn

Menteith   Stirling•

Dunfermline Kinghorn

✕•Dunbar

Dumbarton   Dunipace

(1296)

•Lennox

•Leith

Glasgow•   •Edinburgh

Elderslie• •Bothwell

Lothian

Kyle   •Lanark   •Peebles

Berwick•

Norham•

•Irvine   •Douglas

• •Wark

•Selkirk •Roxburgh

•Jedburgh

•Ayr

Carrick

Northumberland

•Dumfries

ENGLAND

Galloway

•Caerlaverock

Corbridge•

•Carlisle

Cumberland

1–Origins

William Wallace is one of Scotland's most enduring national heroes, commemorated in songs and poems, folklore, monuments, plays and, most recently, in a Hollywood epic. His unrelenting struggle for Scottish freedom from English rule has inspired Scots and many others across the world. He has been portrayed as a patriot, a working-class hero and a real-life Robin Hood despite, or perhaps because of, the extreme scarcity of hard historical evidence. Apart from three letters and one charter, the only contemporary evidence for his life comes from English sources: all the Scottish records from the time have been lost or destroyed. To understand the real William Wallace, it is necessary to peel back the layers of myth and try to get a realistic picture of the man, his life and his times.

Most of the stories we have today concerning William Wallace come from the poem *The Wallace,* written in the late 15th century by Henry the Minstrel (sometimes called *Blind Harry)*, which presents Wallace as the champion of Scotland in an epic struggle against English tyranny. The Minstrel claimed to have based his poem on a Latin biography of Wallace, written in the early 14th century by John Blair, Wallace's chaplain. Unfortunately, no copies of this earlier work have survived, but there are some parallels between *The Wallace* and other older sources; however, the poem should be regarded more as a historical novel than an accurate account of the life of William Wallace.

Born in Elderslie, in Renfrewshire, probably sometime between 1270 and 1275, William Wallace was the second son of Sir Malcolm Wallace. The Wallace family were part of the lower strata of the Scottish ruling classes, holding land granted to them by the powerful Stewarts. Although they did not belong to the first rank of Scottish society, the Wallace family was still an important force. The Stewarts would have depended on their loyalty and support, and William's maternal grandfather was hereditary Sheriff of Ayr, responsible to the King for local administration and government.

As a younger son, William would not inherit his father's lands, and legend has it that he was originally intended for the Church. This is quite possibly true; two of his uncles were priests, in Dunipace and in Dundee. William may indeed have studied with them, learning to read and write, and learning Latin and French as well. It is one of his uncles who reputedly taught him his abiding love of liberty, quoted in this Latin couplet:

> *Dico tibi verum, libertas optima rerum;*
> *Nunquam servili sub nexu vivito, fili.*

(I tell you true, freedom is the best of things; never live within the bonds of slavery, my son). But there is nothing in the limited account of his upbringing that can account for his explosive entry into Scottish political affairs in 1297.

Wallace's story begins near the end of the 13th century, when Scottish nationhood was becoming more defined. The border with England was established and largely agreed upon, and the Treaty of Perth in 1266 acquired the Western Isles from Norway. With a few exceptions, most notably Berwick (originally Scottish, now part of England), Orkney and Shetland (which remained Norwegian possessions until 1468) and the Isle of Man, Scotland's geographical boundaries were much the same as they are today.

The landscape, however, was very different. Today much of the Scottish countryside, particularly in the Lowlands, is made up of open stretches of agricultural land, but in the Middle Ages much of the land was uncultivated. The towns and villages, far smaller than they are today, were ringed with their own little circles of fields; beyond the fields lay a wild countryside of forest, marsh and moor. Rivers and lochs were generally broader and deeper, many of which have disappeared without trace. North of the Forth, the great Caledonian Forest still remained. Unlike the bare hillsides of today, the medieval Highlands were densely forested. Many wild animals roamed there, including wolves and wild boar. Roads were few, and many were little more than simple trackways.

There were also many towns, where the mercantile, commercial and administrative activities of the Kingdom took place. The most successful towns had grown up at important places, such as Stirling, the *gateway to the north*, with its bridge across the

Stirling Castle – protecting the bridge over the Forth.

Forth; at Edinburgh, with its strong fortress and the nearby port of Leith; at Berwick, Scotland's principal trading port; and at St Andrews, a major ecclesiastical centre and place of pilgrimage. Many other towns, such as Inverness, Perth, Dundee, Dunfermline, Dumfries, Roxburgh and Jedburgh, were growing and developing at this time.

The Church was a hugely important institution right across the Christian world in the Middle Ages, with ties and loyalties criss-crossing Europe with little regard for national boundaries. Scotland was no exception. At this time, Scotland had no archbishoprics, and the English church – particularly the Archbishop of York – frequently claimed superiority over their northern counterparts. The Scottish bishops, however, were fiercely protective of their independence from the richer and more

7

powerful English bishops to the south. Deeply involved in the politics and administration of the Kingdom, the Scottish Church was to play a crucial part in Scotland's fight for freedom.

The south and east of Scotland was ruled by nobles and knights, who held their lands of the King and paid their rent in military service. The Highlands and Islands were still dominated by the old Celtic clans; largely inaccessible, they could disregard the King in the Lowlands and often went their own way. Of course, no medieval King could expect total obedience from his subjects. Across Europe, the great nobles were extremely powerful, with large numbers of followers in their own personal armies. Kings remained in power through a complex web of alliances, family ties, friendship and favour, a system which frequently broke down. England, for example, had suffered several baronial revolts in the 13th century, and would endure many more throughout the Middle Ages. The situation in Scotland and England was further complicated by the fact that many nobles held lands on both sides of the Border, and had to swear loyalty to both Kings.

At the time of Wallace's birth this was not a serious problem. Scotland and England had been on good terms for most of the 13th century. Alexander III, King of Scots, and his brother-in-law Edward I, King of England, were friends, and Scotland had prospered during the peace. Many Scottish nobles had fought for Edward, in Wales or against the rebellious English barons. Despite several previous clashes, Scotland and England were not the traditional enemies they were to become; there was every chance that the two Kingdoms could continue in peace as neighbours and friends. But, just as the young William Wallace was entering manhood, Scotland was plunged into crisis. More than three centuries of Anglo-Scottish warfare were about to begin.

Coat of arms of William Wallace

2–A Kingdom in Crisis

On the night of 18 March 1286, a terrible storm was lashing the east coast of Scotland. Such was its ferocity that many feared it heralded some great disaster. But Alexander III, King of Scots, was not a superstitious man. His new French bride, Yolande of Dreux, awaited him at the royal manor of Kinghorn in Fife, across the Firth of Forth, and Alexander was impatient to be with her. Ignoring the advice of his courtiers, he crossed the Forth and set off eagerly along the coast. But in the storm his guides lost touch with him. Alexander never reached his bride; in the morning the King was found dead, his neck broken, lying at the foot of a steep cliff.

Alexander III Monument, Kinghorn

Alexander III had outlived his first wife – Edward I of England's sister Margaret – and all his children. The only remaining direct heir to the Scottish throne was his three-year-old granddaughter Margaret, the *Maid of Norway,* child of Alexander III's own daughter Margaret and her husband, Erik II of Norway. Forty days after the tragedy the great nobles of the realm – bishops, abbots and priors, earls and barons – gathered at Scone to swear loyalty to their infant Queen. Six Guardians were elected – two earls, of Fife and of Buchan; two bishops, of St Andrews and of Glasgow; and two barons, James Stewart and John Comyn – to form a provisional government of the *Community of the Realm of Scotland.*

The realm was far from united, however. Two of the leading

nobles, Robert Bruce, Lord of Annandale (grandfather of the future King), and John Balliol of Galloway, harboured their own claims to the throne. Neither was appointed as a Guardian, but each had three Guardians who supported them – a deliberate arrangement to try and keep the peace. Sensing the possibility of civil war, the Scone parliament sent three envoys to find Edward I, to inform him of the situation and to ask for his advice and protection. Edward agreed. Almost certainly, he saw the opportunity to extend the power and influence of his own royal house over the Maid; his own son, Edward of Caernarvon, was just two years old, and a marriage between the heirs of Scotland and England must have seemed a heaven-sent opportunity. In any union, England would be the dominant partner in both size and wealth and, in any case, he could not risk allowing another royal house – France, for instance – to gain the little Queen and Scotland too. Edward asked for and received a papal bull permitting the marriage, despite the two children being second cousins, and gave King Erik of Norway a personal loan of £2000.

Edward's support was vital to the Guardians, and calmed the potentially volatile situation. Four years of relative peace followed, and in 1290 the Scots signed the Treaty of Birgham, agreeing to the marriage and to the creation of a union of Scotland and England, whilst preserving Scotland as a separate and sovereign realm. But Edward added further assurances of English domination by making the Bishop of Durham his viceroy in Scotland, and in June an English force seized the strategically important Isle of Man. Scotland, however, remained optimistic, preparing for the royal marriage.

In September 1290 the young Queen Margaret set sail from Norway, but during the voyage she fell ill. She died upon reaching Orkney, leaving the succession to the Scottish throne wide open.

The news of the Maid's death sparked a crisis in Scotland. Robert Bruce of Annandale immediately assembled a strong force of men, and John Balliol, now Lord of Galloway, declared himself heir to

Scotland. With civil war looming William Fraser, Bishop of St Andrews, wrote urgently to Edward I, asking him to help decide the Scottish succession and prevent bloodshed.

The Maid's death had dashed Edward's hopes of an easy takeover of Scotland. But perhaps he still had a chance to extend his influence: he invited the Scottish lords and various claimants to Norham Castle in May 1291 and declared that he could only resolve their dispute if they recognised him as supreme overlord of Scotland. After several weeks the representatives replied that they could not answer for any future King, but eventually all the claimants, eager for a decision, agreed to Edward's demands. Their decision may have been aided by the imminent arrival of an English army.

Norham Castle, Northumberland

In June, the Guardians and other Scots lords handed over custody of the country and royal castles to Edward, and he pledged to restore them to the rightful King within two months of his judgement. In August Edward established a court at Berwick which, for the next 18 months, heard and examined all the claims. A total of 13 claimants had come forward, but only four were taken seriously: John Balliol, Lord of Galloway; Robert Bruce, Lord of Annandale; John Hastings of Abergavenny; and Florence V, Count of Holland. All four were direct descendants of Henry, son of David I, King of Scots: the first three through Henry's youngest son David, Earl of Huntingdon, and the fourth through his daughter Ada.

The Count of Holland claimed that David, Earl of Huntingdon had surrendered his and his descendants' claim to the throne in return for lands, but he was unable to prove this. John Hastings claimed that the Kingdom should be divided between the heirs of David of Huntingdon's three daughters, but the first decision of the court was that the Kingdom should remain intact; Edward I, with only one young son and several married daughters, did not wish to set a precedent for splitting Kingdoms. John Balliol claimed through the senior line, through David, Earl of Huntingdon's eldest daughter Margaret. Robert Bruce claimed by nearness of degree: although he was descended from the Earl's second daughter Isabel, he was David's grandson; John Balliol was a great-grandson. Although there was no precedent for such a case, and the principles of inheritance were not firmly defined, most people felt that Balliol's claim was the strongest.

On 17 November 1292, the King of England announced his judgement in favour of John Balliol. King John was enthroned at Scone on St Andrew's Day – 30 November – 1292, and subsequently paid homage to Edward I as his superior lord. Many Scots saw this as a mere formality with no practical consequences; Edward had a different opinion. It was unfortunate in the extreme for Scotland that in a time of crisis they had looked to Edward I for help; although he had always presented a friendly face, he was one of the most ruthless and ambitious monarchs ever to sit on the English throne. One 13th-century English enemy described him as *valiant as a lion, quick to attack the strongest and fearing the onslaught of none. But if a lion in pride and ferocity, he is a leopard in fickleness and inconstancy, changing his word and promise, cloaking himself by pleasant speech. When he is cornered he promises whatever you wish but as soon as he is free he forgets his promise. The treachery or falsehood by which he is advanced he calls prudence; the path by which he attains his ends, however crooked, he calls straight; and whatever he likes be says is lawful.* King Edward would soon become Scotland's greatest enemy.

Edward I quickly took advantage of Balliol's submission to him, and within a week of John's enthronement began to hear appeals from the Scottish court in his own. Several Scottish lords protested that Edward should uphold the treaties which respected the laws and customs of Scotland. Edward's response was to renounce all the promises he made to the Scots during the vacancy of the throne. Scottish opposition to Edward hardened, and King John was persuaded to declare his submission to Edward null and void.

In May 1294 Edward I declared war on France. He called upon the Scottish King, earls and barons, as his vassals, to fight for him, but they refused. He also called upon the Welsh, confidently distributing arms among them. In September, as Edward prepared to sail for Gascony, a rebellion broke out across Wales. The English King was forced to stay and deal with the revolt, which lasted until the following March. Meanwhile, the Scottish nobles decided, despite Balliol's weakness, to fight for Scotland's independence. Although he was still King, Balliol was declared *incompetent* to rule, as if he were a child, and at Stirling in July 1295 they elected a council of 12 to govern the country. By October the council had negotiated a defensive alliance with Edward's enemy, the King of France, ratified in February 1296, effectively declaring war on England.

The Scots issued a call to arms at Caddonlee, near Selkirk in the Borders, for 11 March. Edward I summoned his army to Newcastle and, after Easter, advanced up the eastern route to Berwick. The Scots ravaged south of the Border and tried to take Carlisle, but were thwarted by the Lord of Annandale and the Earl of Carrick. Opposed to Balliol, still harbouring their claim to the Scottish throne, the Bruces placed their loyalties with Edward I.

Facing no opposition, the English army assaulted Berwick on 30 March. Edward gave orders that no life should be spared, and a bloody massacre ensued for two days. The slaughter finally ended when the King himself was repulsed to witness a woman put to the sword during childbirth. The captain of the castle, Sir William Douglas, surrendered himself as a hostage to guarantee the safety of his garrison. Berwick, once the centre of Scotland's commerce, became the headquarters of Edward's Scottish administration.

The Scots retaliated by raiding throughout Northumberland, burning towns, villages and churches and killing indiscriminately. One record describes the burning alive of 200 boys in their school in Corbridge. But their assault was useless: Edward was not going to be distracted from his attack.

Edward marched north to Dunbar. Although her husband was a supporter of Edward, the Countess of Dunbar had, in his absence,

Ruins of Dunbar Castle (1919) – less survives today.

handed the castle to the Scots. On 23 April, English cavalry under John de Warenne, Earl of Surrey, was sent to besiege the castle. After four days, they were attacked by the Scots, under the Earl of Buchan, from the nearby hills. At the sight of the Scottish army, the castle garrison cheered and raised their banners, taunting the English besiegers with the cry, *Tailed dogs, we will cut your tails off!* – it was a popular joke across Medieval Europe that the

English had tails, and was guaranteed to offend.

Warenne led his knights out to meet the attackers. As they approached, the English knights rode down into a valley and out of sight. The Scots assumed that their enemies were fleeing and broke ranks to pursue them. But the English, experienced from warfare in France, were well-ordered and ready to attack. They fell upon the disordered Scots and overwhelmed them in the first charge, sending them fleeing back across the hills. Thousands of foot soldiers, unable to escape, were slaughtered and most of the Scottish nobles were captured.

After Dunbar Edward's progress north was a mere formality. The castles of Roxburgh, Jedburgh and Edinburgh surrendered without resistance, and Stirling was found abandoned – only the porter remained to hand over the keys. In Perth, at Midsummer, Edward received letters of submission from King John. On 8 July, Balliol surrendered in person at Montrose. Edward forced him to resign his Kingdom and renounce the treaty with France, and his seal was broken. Balliol was further humiliated when his royal crest was ripped from his jacket and thrown on the floor. He was afterwards nicknamed *Toom Tabard* – Empty Coat – and he was taken and imprisoned in the Tower of London.

By late July 1296 Edward had reached as far north as Elgin before returning south again. To emphasise his conquest he plundered the royal regalia, including the Black Rood of St Margaret, Scotland's holiest relic, and the Stone of Scone – also called the Stone of Destiny – and sent them to Westminster Abbey. Returning to Berwick, he held a parliament on 28 August where he organised his new Scottish administration and took oaths of fealty from almost all the landholders in Scotland. Over 2000 Scots submitted: the document recording their names became known as the *Ragman Roll* because of the huge number of seals and ribbons attached to it. The government of Scotland was assigned to Englishmen: John de Warenne, Earl of Surrey, was made viceroy; Hugh Cressingham, treasurer; Sir Walter of Amersham, chancellor;

and Sir William Ormesby, chief justice. Notable for their absence from the Ragman Roll are the names of William Wallace, his elder brother Malcolm and his father – an act which made them outlaws in the eyes of the new English administration.

The Bruce family had hoped that, because of their loyalty to Edward, they would now take the throne of Scotland. But Edward was finished with vassal Kings of Scots, and dismissed the Lord of Annandale with the stinging rebuke, *Have we nothing else to do but win kingdoms for you?* As far as Edward was concerned, Scotland was no longer a separate Kingdom, but a province of England.

Scotland was now Edward's land, and Scotland's nobles were either imprisoned in England or paying homage to Edward. English sheriffs and officials were appointed across Scotland, and Scottish castles had English garrisons. Edward must have felt his domination to be total – until, in the words of the chronicler John of Fordun, *William Wallace lifted up his head*.

Map 2: 1296–8 (Chapters 3–5)

3–The Struggle Begins

Why are the names of William Wallace and his family absent from the Ragman Roll, when much of the rest of Scotland – including their direct superior, James Stewart, and all the great nobles – had submitted? Even Wallace's grandfather, Sir Reginald Crawford, had submitted, and kept his position as Sheriff of Ayr. There are several possibilities, not least that they deliberately refused to swear homage. This would have brought them into direct confrontation with William Heselrig, the recently appointed English Sheriff of Lanark, who was responsible for extracting these oaths of loyalty to Edward I from the landholders in his region – which included the Wallace lands of Elderslie. Henry the Minstrel states that Wallace's father, Sir Malcolm senior, was murdered by an English officer named Fenwick for his refusal to do homage. Although there is no other evidence for this, Wallace's father does disappear from the historical record about this time; also, his father's murder would provide a reason for William's implacable hostility to the English.

The very earliest mention of William Wallace recorded anywhere comes from an English court document of 1296, stating that, on 8 August that year, one Matthew of York, in the company of *a thief, one William le Waleys*, stole three shillings' worth of beer from a woman in Perth. Matthew, a cleric, was caught and sentenced to do penance for his crime; his co-accused remained free.

It is by no means certain that this *William le Waleys* is indeed William Wallace of Elderslie, but it is not impossible. Wallace often visited Perth, and knew the area well. Perhaps the young William, having fought for Balliol either at the débâcle at Dunbar or on the futile raid on Northumberland, and unwilling to swear fealty to Edward I, was now living by his wits as a fugitive. Various members of the Wallace family held lands right across Scotland, from Ayrshire and Lanark in the south-west to Moray in the north-east, and he would have been able to call on the help and support of a number of kinsmen.

Henry the Minstrel provides several tales of Wallace's strength, courage and derring-do from this time. In one, English troops tried to help themselves to Wallace's catch while he was fishing, but Wallace attacked and killed three of them before making his escape. In another incident, Wallace eluded his English pursuers by disguising himself as a serving-maid; he sat and spun by the fire while his enemies searched the house in vain. In yet another tale, Wallace is captured – although it took 80 men to do it – and was flung into jail. He was so badly wounded that the jailer thought him dead, and allowed Wallace's old nurse to take the body away for burial. She, of course, tended for Wallace and restored him to health. Some, none or all of these stories may be true or partly true: there is no way of telling. Whatever Wallace did, all we can really know is that he was an outlaw, probably one of many, and individually of little concern to Edward and the English overlords of Scotland. It is what he did in May 1297 that made his name famous across Scotland, and brought it to the attention of the English King.

According to Henry the Minstrel, Wallace had a wife, Marion Braidfoot, who had borne him a daughter. She was also the heiress to the estate of Lamington. William Heselrig had plans to wed Marion to his own son and gain her inheritance, and plotted to dispose of Wallace, sending his henchmen to do the dirty work. They found Wallace and his friend Sir John Graham at mass and unarmed, and pursued them. The two Scots escaped to Marion's house, where they were hastily admitted, then let out the back door, disappearing into the night. Marion, though, was caught by the Sheriff's men and executed, and her house put to the torch.

When William learned of her fate, he called his closest companions – 11 in all – bringing them into Lanark in twos and threes by various gates and assembling them just before nightfall. They approached the Sheriff's house under cover of darkness

The death of William Heselrig

before smashing down the door and bursting in. Heselrig, his son
and his guardsmen were all killed, the Sheriff slain in his bed by
Wallace himself. Such was William's fury that he hacked Heselrig's
body to pieces before setting the building on fire.

21

Marion Braidfoot may or may not have existed; certainly, Wallace had reason enough to hate the Sheriff of Lanark without her. Whatever his motives, the killing of Heselrig was a heavy blow struck against the English overlords. The position of sheriff was vital to the administration of the country, and not just for taxation and law enforcement. First and foremost, sheriffs were responsible for raising and leading the *common army*, the footsoldiers who had always played a prominent role in Scotland's military campaigns. Across Scotland, the English Sheriffs and local officials were being driven out. By the summer of 1297 Cressingham, the English treasurer in Scotland, wrote to the deputy treasurer in London: *Not one of the sheriffs, bailiffs or officials of the Lord King appointed in Scotland can at this time raise a penny of the revenues of their lands, on account of a multitude of different perils which daily and continually threaten them*. Two weeks later he wrote to Edward himself, saying *By far the greater part of your counties in the Scottish Kingdom are still not provided with keepers, because they have been killed, besieged or imprisoned, or have abandoned their bailiwicks and dare not go back. And in some shires the Scots have appointed and established bailiffs and officials*.

Whatever Wallace's personal motives, the murder of Heselrig created a stir across the south-west, and many disaffected men flocked to support him. The chronicler John of Fordun wrote, *From that time there gathered to him all who were of a bitter heart and were weighed down beneath the burden of bondage under the intolerable rule of English domination, and he became their leader*. All over the country, as Cressingham's panicky letters show, the Scots were in revolt. Many of these local uprisings may have been spontaneous; overall, however, there was an organising principle – the Scottish Church.

The Scottish clergy, who had already seen Englishmen appointed to Scottish ecclesiastical positions, were keen to relight the torch of Scottish resistance. All the English chroniclers cite

Robert Wishart, Bishop of Glasgow, as troublemaker-in-chief, and indeed, along with James Stewart, personal supervisor of Wallace himself: *Not daring to break their pledge to the King, they caused a certain bloody man, William Wallace, formerly chief among the brigands of Scotland, to revolt against the King*. As the chronicler suggests, Bishop Wishart, Stewart and other prominent Scotsmen were as yet unwilling to publicly declare their opposition to Edward, but it is certain that they would have encouraged Wallace and other rebels and supported them as best they could.

Meanwhile, in the north-east, another Scottish rebel was making striking progress. Andrew Murray, a young nobleman who, with his father, had been captured at Dunbar, had escaped from his imprisonment in Chester Castle and returned to his family lands in Moray. The Murrays, unlike Wallace, were rich and powerful, holding large tracts of land from Inverness in the north-east to Bothwell in Lanarkshire, and many of their castles had been taken and garrisoned by the English. On his arrival in the north-east, Andrew Murray raised the banner of revolt – always an easy thing to do amongst the wild and unruly men of that district – and proceeded to drive the English out of every fortification from Inverness to Banff. He, too, had strong connections to the Church – his uncle, David Murray, was a priest at Bothwell in 1296; by 1299 he would become Bishop of Moray and Caithness, and an ardent supporter of Scottish independence.

Wallace's band of followers grew rapidly. One of his most notable recruits was Sir William Douglas, captain of Berwick Castle before Edward's bloody assault, brother-in-law to James Stewart and father of James Douglas, who would become one of Robert the Bruce's most famous captains. Apart from his experience and vigorous appreciation of warfare, William Douglas lent authority and respectability to Wallace's small army.

A heavy blow had been struck to the English administration with the death of Heselrig; now Wallace set his sights higher still. Sir

William Ormesby, Edward's justiciar in Scotland, was based at Scone, where previously the Kings of Scots had been inaugurated. No doubt the symbolism of such a location was not lost on Edward or the Scots; the removal of Edward's justiciar would be a major triumph for Wallace.

The attack on Ormesby took place shortly after Heselrig's murder. Wallace and his men rode the 80 miles to Scone Abbey,

Scone Palace, which occupies the site of the Abbey.

and descended upon Ormesby with such little warning that the Englishman barely escaped with his life. He fled Scotland altogether, abandoning a great quantity of valuables, which the jubilant Scots eagerly seized. The fact that Wallace could gather so many horses together for his attack shows the strength of support he received from men like Wishart and Stewart.

Scotland was in open rebellion against English rule. Now, according to an English chronicler, Wallace and his followers *proceeded, not in secret as before, but openly, putting to the sword all the English they could find beyond the Scottish sea, turning themselves afterwards to the siege of castles*. He is said to have taken particular pains to kill or drive out English priests and other members of the clergy; this may be anti-Wallace propaganda on the part of the English chroniclers, or it may reflect the strong backing he received from the Scottish Church. Edward sent orders to the Scottish nobles to suppress the rebellion, but he seems to have misunderstood the situation entirely; many of the nobles now openly declared their hostility to English rule. With Andrew Murray attacking in the north, the MacDuff Earl of Fife in revolt in the east and Wallace rampant in the south and west, the Scottish nobles cast off their oaths to Edward and gathered with their armies at Irvine, near Ayr, in June 1297.

The young Robert Bruce, Earl of Carrick and future King of Scots, was perhaps one Scottish noble who had nothing to gain and everything to lose from the restoration of John Balliol. And yet even he, whose father and grandfather had refused to fight for Balliol in 1296, joined with the Scots at Irvine. Ordered by Edward and his own father to attack Douglasdale to punish William Douglas for his support of Wallace, Bruce mustered his men and told them, *No man holds his flesh and blood in hatred and I am no exception. I must join my own people and the nation in which I was born. Choose then whether you go with me or return to your homes.*

Despite this and other similar sympathies from the other Scottish nobles, the gathering at Irvine was a rather inept and half-hearted affair. Two prominent northern English barons, Henry Percy and Robert Clifford, alarmed by this open show of revolt, had gathered a powerful body of knights and crossed the Border, reaching Ayr Castle by the end of June. When they saw the English force arrayed against them, the brittle self-confidence of the Scottish nobles shattered, and they immediately began negotiations for surrender. One Scottish knight, Sir Richard Lundie, was so disgusted by this he promptly changed sides.

Here was a clash of two different kinds of warfare. Richard Lundie was a chivalric knight, to whom combat was honourable and negotiation contemptible, regardless of the ultimate outcome. The Scottish nobles would have had a lot of sympathy with this idea; however, they had lands and power to protect, and were caught up in the murky world of national and international politics. They knew that, in England, Edward was in difficulty: he was in dispute with both the English Church and with several of his most powerful earls and barons, and there was a real possibility of civil war. Beyond them was a third type of warfare: Wallace and his followers, beholden to no-one, fighting for a cause – the survival of the Kingdom of Scots.

Wallace's sword – preserved at the Wallace Monument, near Stirling.

4–The Battle of Stirling Bridge

Although many Scottish nobles did eventually promise to submit to Edward, few of them kept their pledges. William Douglas was imprisoned in Berwick Castle, where he was *very savage and abusive* until his death a year later. Bishop Wishart was imprisoned in Roxburgh Castle. Robert Bruce and James Stewart

Shattered ruins of Roxburgh Castle (1917)

remained at large, although Edward deprived them of their estates. Despite the less than glorious performance of the Scots lords at Irvine, they did gain something: time. By spinning out the negotiations for surrender for almost a month, they gave Wallace and Murray freedom to conduct their campaigns against the occupying English forces.

Edward, meanwhile, was trying desperately to raise an English army to fight in Flanders against the French. Facing hostility from many of his own barons, he decided to release a number of the Scottish nobles captured at Dunbar, on the condition that they return to their Scottish lands and quell the disturbances there before following him overseas. On arrival in Scotland, these Scottish lords saw for themselves the true scale of the uprising;

they contented themselves with sending loyal messages of support to Edward, remaining inactive and awaiting developments. One English chronicler states that *even when they were with the King in body, their hearts were with the Scots.*

By August Murray had gained undisputed control of the north-east, and Wallace had driven the English out of Fife and Perthshire. The two armies had met and joined together somewhere in the Tay valley, and, taking the town of Dundee, besieged the castle. We do not know what their meeting was like. Murray was a nobleman, from one of the oldest and most powerful Scottish families; Wallace, while hardly a commoner, was still socially inferior. And yet there is no sign of any dispute between the two men, and no indication of any conflict over command or rank. Wallace and Murray, despite their social differences, were two young men fighting side by side for the same cause.

Edward felt secure enough by 22 August to depart for Flanders, still confident that his knights and noblemen could deal with the Scottish insurrection. At long last Warenne, his viceroy in Scotland, who had spent most of his time on his English estates, stirred himself into action. He marshalled a formidable force, probably 600 cavalry and 20 000 infantry, many of them Welsh, to face a Scottish force of around 5000 footsoldiers with perhaps 150 horsemen. Warenne, an old soldier, knew the tremendous power of his heavily armed and armoured knights, and confidently assumed that their natural superiority would sweep away the common Scottish rabble. Linking up with Cressingham, the corpulent English treasurer – nicknamed the *treacherer* by the Scots – Warenne and the English army marched to Stirling.

With its powerful castle – one of only a handful remaining in English hands – and its bridge crossing the Forth, Stirling was the key to the control of Scotland. Hearing of the English approach, Wallace and Murray assembled their men and marched to intercept them, prepared to confront the armed might of England.

Despite the overwhelming odds, this was not an act of foolhardy bravado. Wallace and Murray knew that the English army would have to cross Stirling Bridge to reach them. More importantly, they would have to cross the causeway that ran for half a mile from the northern end of the bridge across a broad swathe of soft, boggy ground. The heavy English cavalry would be forced to keep to the causeway, where they could ride no more than two abreast. There, unable to launch their shattering charge, they would be vulnerable. Accordingly, the Scots took up position on the slopes of the Abbey Craig, overlooking the causeway, to await the arrival of the English.

Although the Scottish leaders had chosen their ground well, the conventional wisdom of the day was that footsoldiers could not stand against mounted knights, no matter what the terrain – the knights' superiority came from their noble blood as much as from their arms and armour. By this time, most of the Scottish nobles – with the notable exception of Andrew Murray – were ostensibly supporters of Edward I.

Wallace Monument, Abbey Craig – near where Wallace marshalled his forces for the battle.

On 9 September 1297, James Stewart and Malcolm, Earl of Lennox, at the head of a group of Scottish lords, approached Warenne and offered to parley with the Scottish army, to negotiate their surrender. Much of the Scottish army was made up of men from their lands, acting independently of their lords, and it is not unreasonable to assume that Stewart and the others wished to prevent the wholesale slaughter of their vassals. Cressingham, hungry for glory, protested, but Warenne, perhaps wanting a quick return to his southern estates, agreed.

The Scottish nobles made their way towards the Scottish camp. There they met with Murray and Wallace, possibly pointing out the overwhelming size of the English force, their massive superiority in arms and armour and the futility of trying to resist. In all probability they would have pleaded with them to disperse, to await a better time. But Wallace and Murray were defiant; the English army had invaded, and the army of the community of the realm of Scotland would resist them. Stewart, Lennox and the other nobles returned to the English camp on 10 September and confessed their failure to Warenne. Perhaps as a token of their good faith, and more importantly to associate themselves with what they saw as the winning side, they offered to join the English army the next day with 40 knights.

On the evening of 10 September, Warenne informed his army at their camp near Stirling Castle that they would cross the bridge the following morning and engage the Scots. At first light, the English army mustered. Warenne, however, possibly taking advantage of the more comfortable accommodation offered by Stirling Castle, slept in, causing confusion and delay among his troops and irritating the impatient Cressingham. Finally he arose, and then caused further delay by insisting on the chivalric tradition of creating several new knights. Cressingham, no doubt, fumed quietly as each solemn ritual was enacted. Meanwhile, Stewart, Lennox and the other Scottish nobles had returned to the English camp, but they brought no followers with them: none could be persuaded to come.

Yet again, Warenne delayed. He sent two Dominican friars to the Scots, to give them one final chance to surrender. It must have been a lonely and nerve-wracking journey across the narrow wooden bridge and along the causeway towards the Scottish army. They met with Wallace and Murray, and put to them Warenne's demand for surrender. Wallace gave them the same reply he had given to Stewart and the Scots lords: *Tell your commander that we are not here to make peace, but to do battle to defend ourselves and liberate our Kingdom. Let them come on, and we will prove this in their very beards.*

As the Dominican friars reported their failure to Warenne, one knight spoke up. Sir Richard Lundie, the Scot who had joined the English camp in disgust at Irvine, had seen the danger of crossing the bridge and causeway in the teeth of the Scottish army. *My lord,* he said, *if we cross that bridge now, we are dead men. For we can only go over two abreast, and the enemy are already formed up: they can charge down on us whenever they wish. There is a ford not far from here, where 60 men can cross at a time. Give me 500 horsemen, then, and a small body of footsoldiers, and we will attack the Scots from behind: then the rest of the army will be able to cross the bridge in perfect safety.*

This was a crucial moment: if the English had followed Lundie's advice and crossed the Forth at the Fords of Drip, a few miles upstream, it is doubtful that the Scots could have resisted them. However, it was here that Cressingham's patience finally broke, and he exclaimed *It will do us no good, my lord earl, either to go bickering like this or to waste the King's money in vain manoeuvres. So let us cross right away, and do our duty as we are bound to do.* Warenne made a fatal mistake and agreed with Cressingham. After all, the Scottish army they faced was made up only of peasant footmen; what threat could they pose to the flower of English chivalry? He gave the order to begin the crossing.

The eager Cressingham took the position of honour, commanding the English vanguard. Slowly, two abreast, the English knights began to file onto the bridge and along the narrow causeway. With their banners and pennons, their bright armour, their surcoats and horse-trappings, they made a colourful cavalcade in the September

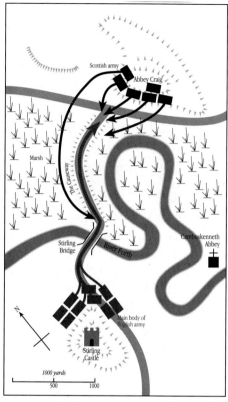

As the English advance, the Scots seize both ends of the Causeway, trapping their enemies north of the Forth.

sunshine. Wallace and Murray, on the slopes of the Abbey Craig, watched and waited.

Then, when the head of the English van had almost reached firm ground, they sounded the charge. The Scottish soldiers, armed for the most part with 12-foot-long spears, swept down the slope and crashed into the narrow front of the English force, throwing it back onto the men behind. More Scots soldiers began to pour down both sides of the causeway, picking their way across the marshy ground and lapping down either side of the English

32

The Battle of Stirling Bridge

column. Unable to defend themselves, the knights and their horses were easy targets for the Scottish spearmen.

Rearing and plunging, many horses were driven off the causeway into the treacherous marshland. Floundering in the soft ground, they were helpless prey to the surrounding Scots. Knights fell or were dragged from their horses to be stabbed where they lay, long daggers thrust through their visors and chinks in their encumbering armour. Panic swept through the English forces; those who could regained the bridge, trying to force their way back against the press of their comrades. A picked body of

Scottish spearmen, possibly commanded by Murray, quickly crossed the marsh and took the bridgehead, sealing the trap. The English forces on the southern bank could only watch as the slaughter continued. The causeway had become a killing ground.

The English vanguard now had only one thought: escape. Many of the Welsh infantrymen who had crossed the bridge abandoned their weapons and flung themselves into the river. Those

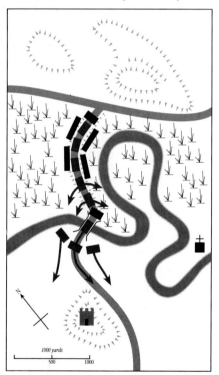

Attacked on both flanks, and unable to defend themselves, the English knights are surrounded and destroyed.

knights who could stripped off their armour and followed them; others, less fortunate, still wore their mail when they were driven into the Forth, to be dragged down and drowned. One English knight, Sir Marmaduke Tweng, fought free, charging through the Scottish blockade to the bridge and safety. Others were not so lucky: an uncounted number of English and Welsh footmen and well over 100 knights were slain, amongst them the impatient Cressingham. His body was flayed by the victorious Scots, and pieces of his skin sent around the country as tokens of their triumph. Wallace himself took enough to make a new sword belt. Warenne, who had remained in impotent safety on the southern side, led the remainder of his army in flight, pausing only to place the captaincy of Stirling Castle into the hands of Sir Marmaduke Tweng and Sir William FitzWarin; they replaced Sir Richard Waldegrave, who had fallen in the battle. Warenne himself headed rapidly southwards, not stopping until he reached Berwick. Many other English lords and knights followed suit, abandoning the heavy wagons in the baggage train. The English rank and file, the wagon-teams and other camp followers, did not fare so well. They tried to make their escape towards Falkirk, passing by a wooded, marshy area known as *The Pows*. Unfortunately for them, James Stewart and the other Scots lords, when they saw the tide of battle turn against the English, had quietly withdrawn from the field and were skulking here with their retinues under cover of the trees. As the English baggage train passed, the Scottish nobles, fired with a sudden patriotic fervour, emerged from the woodland and fell upon them. The English camp followers scattered, many being ridden down and killed, and much of the supply train was taken as booty: an important, if inglorious, contribution to the Scottish victory.

Stirling Bridge was a shattering defeat for the English. Although it was not, in the long term, a decisive victory for the Scots, it was the nature of the defeat that was so shocking. An army of mounted knights, socially as well as militarily superior to the Scottish forces that opposed them, had been cut to pieces; to the people of the time, such an event was unparalleled, almost against nature. At Dunbar, the Scots nobles had behaved as if warfare was a sport. At Stirling Bridge, an army of the poor commonality of Scotland had shown that they would not play by the rules and customs of their lords: they would fight tooth and nail for their freedom.

Stirling Bridge – this 15th-century bridge stands near the site of the battle.

5–Scotland's Champion

In the immediate aftermath of the battle, there was much to be done. It fell to Wallace to take these first important steps; Andrew Murray had been seriously wounded in the battle. The castles of Dundee and Stirling still remained in English hands, although when news of the Scottish victory reached Dundee the garrison immediately surrendered. More importantly, the garrison at Stirling offered to surrender also, if their lives were spared. Sir Marmaduke Tweng, Sir William FitzWarin and others were taken and imprisoned in Dumbarton Castle. Freed in an exchange of

Dumbarton Castle – not much remains of the medieval castle on its rock.

prisoners in 1299, Sir Marmaduke lived on to fight at Bannockburn, where once again he came through unscathed.

Except for isolated garrisons in the south and east, no English soldiers remained in Scotland. John Balliol, King of Scots, was imprisoned in England, but his realm had broken free from England's grasp. Suddenly, Wallace was flung into very unfamiliar territory. He had led small bands of men on midnight raids; he had commanded larger forces of men, criss-crossing the countryside to attack garrisons; and with Murray, he had commanded an army and led them to victory. Now there was a Kingdom to govern in the name of King John.

Fortunately for Wallace, the Scottish Church, always the administrative engine of the Kingdom, was behind him. Only a month after the battle, official letters were sent overseas proclaiming Scotland's independence. One surviving letter, sent to the mayors and communes of the German trading towns of Lübeck and Hamburg, informed them that their merchants could have *safe access to all the parts of the realm of Scotland with their merchandise; for the realm of Scotland, thank God, has been recovered by war from the dominion of the English*. The letter was signed *Andrew Murray and William Wallace, commanders of the army of the realm of Scotland, and the community of the same realm*. Despite the unprecedented circumstances, the forms and practices of the Kingdom could continue.

Southern Scotland suffered badly in 1296 and 1297: food stocks had been taken by marauding English armies, and many fields were left unplanted and crops unharvested. It was to this pressing practical concern that Wallace now turned his hand. Leaving the administration of the realm in the hands of the Church – and to those Scottish lords who had now thrown off their allegiance to Edward – he organised a massive punitive raid on the north of England.

He mustered his army at Roslin Moor in Lothian and marched south, crossing into England on 18 October. The English merchants in Roxburgh and Berwick fled before him, spreading panic across Northumberland. Wallace's men ravaged the countryside, plundering the stores of food and rounding up cattle and other livestock. The Scots were savage and ferocious, killing, looting and burning indiscriminately, driving the terrified English in front of them. One English chronicler states that *the service of God ceased totally in all the monasteries and churches between Newcastle and Carlisle, for all the canons, monks and priests fled before the face of the Scots, as did nearly all the people*. All across northern England, from Cockermouth in the west to Newcastle in the east, the Scots raided unopposed.

At Hexham Abbey, three clergymen were discovered by a party of Scots, who demanded that they produce the Abbey's treasures. They answered that everything of value had already been stolen by other Scots. Before events took a nasty turn, Wallace arrived. Dismissing the intruders, he asked the clergymen to celebrate mass. After the elevation of the Host, Wallace, as custom demanded, left the

Hexham Abbey, Northumberland

Abbey to lay down his weapons. In his absence the marauding Scots returned and stole the chalice, the altar ornaments, the prayer book and even the altar cloths. When Wallace returned the anguished priest informed him what had happened. Wallace declared that the thieves should be caught and hanged, but his troops made little or no attempt to find them – an attitude that Wallace must have expected. Apologising for the bad character of his men, he issued the Abbey with a letter of protection under the authority of *Andrew Murray and William Wallace, commanders of the army of Scotland, in the name of the renowned Prince, Lord John, by the grace of God illustrious King of Scotland*.

Crossing over to Carlisle, Wallace challenged the garrison of the castle to surrender, but the English troops, safe behind the thick walls of that grim fortress, defied him. Lacking any siege engines, and preferring not to engage in a long and possibly fruitless siege, Wallace and his troops marched away, turning southwards to menace the rich city of Durham.

On 11 November, as they approached Durham, the weather

took a dramatic turn for the worse, bringing sudden storms of snow and hail. The people of Durham took this to be a miraculous intervention by St Cuthbert, whose bones were buried in Durham Cathedral. Taking heart, they rose up and presented the Scots with the only serious resistance of the entire raid, marching in some numbers to oppose them. Weighed down with booty, buffeted by the icy winds and perhaps fearful of St Cuthbert's wrath, the Scots abandoned their assault and marched away again.

Winter was closing in, and Wallace had pressing concerns at home. Turning back, he carried out one last raid along the Tyne valley before crossing the Border into Scotland. The northern counties of England had felt his wrath; the name of Wallace was stamped firmly on the memories of the inhabitants.

Wallace was back in Scotland before the end of November, where, in the midst of victory, he received some sorrowful news: Andrew Murray was dead. Wallace would have to bear the burden of government alone. But how could William Wallace, a man described by one English source as *a landless squire*, impose his will on the great lords of Scotland? The answer lay in the changing nature of the *Community of the Realm*. In 1286, Guardians had been appointed to rule the Kingdom in the absence of a monarch, in the name of the Community of the Realm of Scotland – essentially, the nobles, knights and bishops. But at Stirling Bridge the people of Scotland had shown that they would sooner follow Wallace than their own liege lords, and without the support of the common army the nobles were powerless. No government can rule without the consent – or at least the tolerance – of the general population; having raised their voices, the commonality had claimed their place in the Community of the Realm.

Wallace was also helped by the fundamental splits which still divided the Scottish lords. Two great power blocks existed: the Comyns, related to Balliol and loyal to his name; and the Bruces, still harbouring their claim to the throne of Scotland. Wallace represented a middle way. Although he acted in King John's name, he was closely tied to the Stewarts, staunch supporters of Bruce; his uncle, Sir Richard Wallace, was married to a Bruce; and his brother, Sir Malcolm, was in Bruce's service. Wallace had won his authority on the field of battle, of great symbolic importance to the lords as well as to the common people. Finally, from the earliest days of his career, he had the support of the Scottish Church.

Wallace understood the importance of the Church's backing and acted accordingly. Bishop Fraser of St Andrews had died in France on 20 August 1297. On 3 November, on Wallace's instructions, William Lamberton, Chancellor of Glasgow Cathedral and a

Glasgow Cathedral – crypt and St Mungo's tomb

staunch supporter of the Scottish cause, was elected as the new Bishop. Many years previously, in an attempt to end English claims of superiority, the Scottish Church had been made a *Special Daughter of the Pope*: essentially, the Pope was to be Archbishop of Scotland. Unfortunately, this meant that new Scottish bishops had to travel to Rome to be consecrated – a difficult journey in peacetime made doubly difficult by English hostility. Nevertheless,

Wallace is knighted.

Lamberton embarked for France sometime in late 1297 or early 1298, braving storms and English ships, and thence to Rome where he was consecrated on 1 June 1298. Both there and in France he was to provide invaluable diplomatic support for the Scottish cause.

Wallace turned his attention to the nobles, most of whom were willing to give him at least tacit support. Despite their internal divisions, and Wallace's lower status, they would follow him – a telling tribute to the remarkable force of his personality and the driving passion with which he pursued his cause. There was only one problem: Wallace was not a knight. The institution of knighthood was so strong that even a King had to be knighted before he could truly rule. So, in March 1298, in the Ettrick Forest, Wallace was knighted by *a prominent man of the Scottish race* – quite possibly Robert Bruce, the future King. The institution of guardianship was resurrected, this time under one man. From this date his edicts were issued in the name of *William Wallace, Knight, Guardian of the Kingdom of Scotland and commander of its armies, in the name of the renowned Prince, Lord John, by the grace of God illustrious King of Scotland, by consent of the Community of that realm.*

Map 3: 1298–1305 (Chapters 6–9)

6–The Battle of Falkirk

In England, Wallace's victory at Stirling Bridge and his raid on the northern counties caused shock and outrage. The barons and earls ceased their squabbling and made their peace with their King, soon to return from Flanders. Wallace was vilified as a thief and a brigand, a monstrous ogre who would force nuns to dance naked in front of him, a murderer and a coward. When Edward arrived back in England in the spring of 1298, he found his Kingdom united behind him against the Scots. Edward's temper can hardly have been improved when the Scottish nobles, captured at Dunbar and serving under him in Flanders, deserted at Aardenburg and joined the French. Bent on the subjugation of Scotland, he transferred his seat of government to York and summoned a massive army to assemble at Roxburgh on 25 June. Calling together some 2000 cavalry and 12 000 infantry – 10 000 of whom were Welsh or Irish – Edward joined his army in early July.

The English forces marched northwards through Lauderdale, burning and destroying as they went, without finding any sign of a Scottish army. By 11 July they were on the outskirts of Edinburgh, and running into trouble: food transports due at Leith were delayed, and those that had arrived held more wine than food. The English also learned that three of the formidable fortresses on his eastern flank – Dirleton, Dunbar and possibly Hailes – were in the hands of the Scots. Edward sent the Bishop of Durham and a large body of men to capture them, but the Bishop – who had no siege engines and whose men were living off beans and peas scavenged from the fields – could make no progress. He sent Sir John FitzMarmaduke to Edward for fresh instructions. Edward told him, *Go back and tell the bishop that he is a man of Christian piety, but Christian piety has no place in what he is now doing. As for you, Sir John, you are a bloodthirsty man. I have often had to rebuke you for being too cruel. Now be off, and use your cruelty, and instead of rebuking you I shall praise you. Do not return*

Dirleton Castle – see previous page

until all three castles are burned. Sir John returned with his grim message. As he reached his forces, food ships suddenly arrived. Heartened, the English troops renewed their attacks and two days later the castles surrendered.

Meanwhile, the main body of Edward's army was nearing starvation. Edward, trying to boost morale, issued them with wine – a very dangerous move. Many of the Welsh footsoldiers became violently drunk and engaged in a large-scale brawl with their English counterparts, killing several of them. A group of English knights then charged the Welshmen, slaying 80 and routing the rest. The next morning Edward was told that the Welsh were threatening to join with the Scots against him: *Let them go if they please*, said Edward, *with God's grace I shall be avenged on them both in one day*. The angry Welshmen decamped and remained at a distance, declaring that if the Scots should gain the upper hand, they would join with them against the English.

Seeing that his expedition was in danger of collapse, Edward decided to retreat to Edinburgh. Just then his luck changed. Sir John FitzMarmaduke arrived to tell him of his success; the English supply ships, entering the waters of the Forth, hove into view; and Patrick, Earl of Dunbar and a prominent supporter of the English, brought news that Wallace and his men were camped only 13 miles away, near Falkirk. Suddenly the English morale lifted; the Welshmen, in dire need of supplies, rejoined the army and Edward, mounting his horse, led his troops westwards to Linlithgow.

With the Scots nearby, the English slept in full armour, Edward sleeping like his men on the ground next to his horse. In the night, the King's horse trod on him, breaking one of his ribs; but Edward, determined now to engage the enemy, insisted on mounting his horse to lead his men. Shortly after dawn, English scouts saw many Scottish troops lining the crest of a hill, the sunlight glittering on their spear-points. But as the army approached the Scotsmen disappeared into the hills.

Despite having defeated them once before, Wallace knew and feared the terrible force of the English cavalry, and had deliberately avoided making contact with the enemy. His plan had been to draw the English on, stretching out their supply lines and allowing hunger and internal strife to do its work – a strategy which had very nearly succeeded. Stirling Bridge had been a unique opportunity which he could not dare hope for again. His army – made up of around 6000 footsoldiers equipped with long spears, a small body of archers from the Ettrick Forest, and perhaps 500 or 600 knights contributed by the nobles – was no match in the open field for Edward's host. Unfortunately, many voices in the Scottish army, emboldened by their recent success, demanded that they stand and fight. Wallace, whose authority largely rested on the support of the army, had to give way.

Choosing his position with care, Wallace sited his army on the south-eastern slope of Slamman hill, protected at the front by a large bog formed by the junction of the Hallglen and Westquarter

burns. On top of the hill and to their rear was the Callendar Wood.
He arranged his spearmen into four schiltrons, closely-packed
circles of between 1000–2000 men each. With the butts of the long
spears planted firmly on the ground, their iron tips fanning
upwards and outwards, these hedgehog-like formations provided
a formidable defence against charging horsemen. Wooden stakes
were planted at an angle all around each schiltron and roped
together to provide further protection. Between the schiltrons
stood the archers, with the cavalry on the crest of the hill behind.
Having made his preparations for this unlooked-for battle, Wallace
turned to his men: *I have brought you to the ring*, he told them,
hop if you can.

The Scots did not have long to wait. As soon as Edward's army
sighted them the English cavalry plunged into the attack,
disregarding their King's orders to pause to feed their men. On
the left the vanguard under the earls of Norfolk, Hereford and
Lincoln charged forward, only sighting the intervening marsh at
the last minute and swinging left to avoid it. On the right the rest
of the cavalry, under the nominal command of the Bishop of
Durham, swept forward and right. Sweeping around both sides of

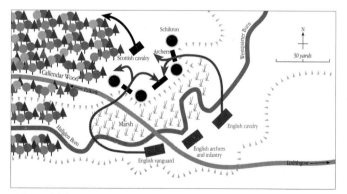

*The English knights charge, overwhelming the Ettrick archers and driving off the
Scottish cavalry, but are unable to break up the close-packed schiltrons.*

the marsh, they crashed back through the Scottish formations and rode down the Ettrick archers, killing them almost to a man. The Scottish cavalry, with memories of Dunbar all too fresh in their minds, broke and ran, flying the field without striking a blow. But the tightly-packed schiltrons stood firm, resisting the repeated charges of the English knights and killing many of their horses.

Edward must have been furious. He had finally, with much labour, brought the Scots to battle, and now his knights in their lust for blood and glory threatened to destroy themselves on the Scottish spears. Somehow over the din of battle he managed to get them to withdraw a little distance to let his archers, Welsh longbowmen and foreign crossbowmen, do their work. Arrows and bolts poured into the schiltrons, and the Scottish soldiers fell in their hundreds. Still they held their formations, as their ranks thinned and the dense hedges of spears began to evaporate.

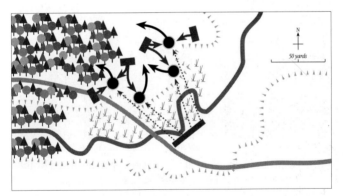

Edward I orders his cavalry to break off, and his archers unleash volleys of arrows into the Scottish formations. The cavalry charge again, and the schiltrons are shattered.

Finally, Edward signalled his cavalry to charge again. Unable to resist, the schiltrons broke and the Scots were scattered. Hundreds, perhaps thousands, of Scots died in the massacre that followed. Wallace himself barely escaped, fleeing with a core of followers into the surrounding woodland. But Falkirk was not another Dunbar; here there was no general surrender. Although Edward had won a crushing victory, Scotland was far from subdued.

Edward's northward progress halted at Stirling after the castle was recaptured, and all of Scotland north of the Forth still remained outside his grasp. He remained in Stirling for two weeks while his ribs healed, before marching into Fife. He reached St Andrews, but found it and the rest of the countryside deserted. He

St Andrews Castle – the now-ruined stronghold of the Bishops of St Andrews.

turned towards Perth, but that had already been destroyed by the Scots themselves, possibly on Wallace's orders. Returning southwards, Edward made a detour to the south-west in pursuit of Robert Bruce. But when he reached Ayr, towards the end of August, he found a deserted town and a burnt-out castle, destroyed on Bruce's orders. By the end of September, Edward was in England again, having managed to capture Lochmaben Castle – his only success after his victory at Falkirk.

Shortly after his escape from Falkirk, Wallace ceased to be Guardian of Scotland. This, perhaps, was Edward's greatest achievement of 1298. It is not known whether Wallace resigned or was forced to step down. The 14th-century chronicler, John of Fordun, states that after Falkirk, *which was vouchsafed for the enemy through the treachery of Scots* (the noble cavalry), *William Wallace, perceiving by these and other strong proofs the glaring wickedness of the Comyns and their abettors, chose rather to serve with the crowd than to be set over them. So, not long after the battle, he, of his own accord, resigned the office and charge of Guardian.* Fordun was of course writing after the later destruction of the Comyns by Bruce, and was careful to portray them as the enemies of Scotland. However, the headlong retreat of the Scottish cavalry at the start of the battle was not due to treachery. Hopelessly outnumbered, they could not stand against the English knights; the only contribution they could have made would have been to assist the pursuit of the English in the event of a Scottish victory.

Wallace had become Guardian through the support of the common army of Scotland and by the strength of his own personality. Unlike Dunbar, the defeat at Falkirk was not a rout; Wallace managed to retreat in good order with a body of troops. Indeed, one account of the battle tells of the English pursuit of Wallace, and credits him with the killing of Sir Brian le Jay, Master of the English Templars and the only notable English casualty of the battle. Luring le Jay and his knights into a marsh, Wallace and his men turned back on the English and destroyed them. If Wallace had asked them for their support, the ordinary soldiers of Scotland would have given it: however, he probably chose to step down from command. Despite their ineffectiveness at Falkirk, the nobles had at last been galvanised into positive and public action against Edward. These men were by birth the natural leaders of medieval Scotland; Wallace had by his actions and example spurred them into choosing sides and making a stand.

7–War and Diplomacy

One thing that we can be sure Wallace did was to help enforce the resistance to English rule. He was a driven man, and he drove others before him too. Noble or common, rich or poor, Wallace would go to any lengths to force the people of Scotland to fight for their freedom. When he issued his summons to arms prior to Falkirk, Wallace ordered gibbets to be constructed in every parish in the country as a stern reminder of the punishment for non-compliance. Landowners were warned to expect imprisonment and the confiscation of their lands if they tried to prevent their tenants from joining him. In the spring of 1298, Wallace is said to have journeyed north to deal with *certain recalcitrants*, and to have hanged several who defied him. Although he was no longer Guardian, William Wallace was still a force to be reckoned with, and it is certain that he continued to use all his energies to uphold the cause for Scottish independence.

In this he was successful. Sometime between August and December 1298, two new Guardians were appointed, drawn this time from the ranks of the nobility: Robert Bruce, Earl of Carrick, and John Comyn of Badenoch. This of course was a direct reflection of the factional split that ran through the Scottish nobility, and was without doubt an uneasy alliance. But the credit for the creation of this union, impossible in 1297, must go to the example and inspiration of Wallace. This was a continuation of independent government, which recognised and confirmed the rulings and appointments made by Wallace, and acted to restore and extend Scottish rule in the name of King John. By November 1299, the isolated English garrison at Stirling had been starved into submission – they had been reduced to eating their horses – and sheriffs and other officials loyal to Scotland were appointed to areas previously under English rule. Wallace played his part in all this; he was credited by the English with cutting off the supply route to Stirling Castle.

Stirling Castle – see previous page

If 1298 had been a bad year militarily for the Scots, they did manage to achieve some important diplomatic successes. William Lamberton, whom Wallace had appointed as Bishop of St Andrews, had worked hard for the Scottish cause in both the French and papal courts: as early as June and July 1298 Philip IV of France and Pope Boniface VIII had both written to Edward, urging him to release Balliol and to cease his attacks on Scotland. In the spring of 1299 the Guardians sent further envoys to the King of France, who wrote back to them with warmth and friendship, recalling the Franco-Scottish treaty of 1295–6, stating himself *moved to the very marrow by the evils brought on their country through hostile malignancy*, and praising them *for their constancy to their King and their shining valour in defence of their native land against injustice*. Although Philip was not sufficiently moved to give in to Lamberton's request for an expeditionary force of French knights, the support of the most powerful monarch in Europe – to whom Edward owed homage as Duke of Aquitaine – was invaluable.

By June 1299 the Pope wrote to the Archbishop of Canterbury

condemning in the strongest terms the English assaults on
Scotland and, declaring Scotland to be subject to the Papacy, he
demanded that the entire Anglo-Scottish conflict be laid before
him for final judgement. Edward was conscious of the weight of
international opinion against him, and of his own domestic
problems. He had been unable to muster an army to campaign in
Scotland in the summer of 1299, as he had planned to do after
Falkirk. So, in July, Balliol was released from England and handed
over to the French, on the condition that he be kept in papal
custody.

This was an enormous breakthrough. Before, with Balliol
imprisoned in England, there can have been no real chance of his
restoration. Now, under intense diplomatic pressure, the first
cracks in Edward's power were appearing. It must have seemed to
the Scots that, if they could not win their freedom outright by
force of arms, right could triumph over might with the aid of
friends overseas. As Lamberton returned to Scotland in July 1299,
Wallace himself resolved to undertake a new diplomatic mission,
principally to France and Rome.

At first, it may seem strange that a man of such military energy
should resort to diplomacy. However, there are good reasons
behind his actions. First, he had driven the Scottish nobles to take
a stand and showed them that the Scottish people would not
tolerate English rule. Second, he had fired their own sense of
patriotism, making them see that the land of their birth was more
valuable to them than their estates in England, and causing such
enemies as the Bruces and the Comyns to make common cause.
Third, he may have felt that he was perhaps in the way, that his
presence in Scotland was in some respects causing divisions
amongst the Scottish people. Although no longer Guardian, many
people in Scotland remembered defying their lords and emerging
victorious at Stirling Bridge, and many others would have had
cause to resent the flight of the nobles, however sensible, at

Falkirk. Wallace still commanded a great deal of support and loyalty, and his refusal to align himself with either the Bruce or the Comyn faction would have made both parties suspicious of him.

This suspicion spilled over in an incident at a council held by the Guardians at Peebles on 12 August, just as Wallace was preparing to depart for the Continent. We have a peculiarly reliable account of this event, from a report made to the English Constable of Roxburgh by an English spy. At the council, one Sir David Graham, a follower of John Comyn, demanded that he be given Wallace's lands and goods, as he was leaving Scotland *without the leave or approval of the Guardians*. Sir Malcolm Wallace, William's brother and a follower of Bruce, hotly refused this claim, stating that his brother's possessions were *protected by the peace in which Wallace had left the Kingdom, since he was leaving to work for the good of the Kingdom*. Daggers were drawn and a fight ensued. Hearing that their supporters were fighting, and perhaps jumping to conclusions, John Comyn leapt at Bruce and seized him by the throat. With some difficulty, Bishop Lamberton and James Stewart managed to separate the combatants, but the damage was done. Although Bruce and Comyn remained for the moment as Guardians, with Lamberton appointed as a third, neutral Guardian, the split was too deep to be permanently patched up. By the spring of 1300, Bruce had resigned.

William Wallace was not present at Peebles; indeed, he may already have departed. Here his movements become obscure indeed. Henry the Minstrel tells us of encounters with French and English pirates, whom Wallace respectively overawed and killed. We are also told that Wallace so impressed King Philip of France that he was offered the lordship of Guyenne, which of course he declined. There is also an account of a hand-to-hand struggle with an enraged lion, in which Wallace was again victorious.

The documented facts are more mundane, but are so scanty that his actual movements can only be guessed at. He had a letter of safe-conduct from Haakon V, King of Norway; it is possible that he visited that country, to remind the King of his ties to Scotland and to enlist his aid against Edward, although the letter may have only been for a visit to the Norwegian-held Orkney Islands. Wallace did visit France, possibly on more than one occasion, and received a letter from Philip IV, describing him as *our beloved William le Walois of Scotland, knight,* instructing the French representatives at the papal court to aid and support him. Wallace did travel to Rome, quite possibly meeting Balliol either there or on the way; although what that lack-lustre and ineffectual monarch thought of William Wallace, or of Scotland, from the comfort of France is hard to imagine.

Much of the activity of the Scottish diplomats was legalistic, and regardless of Wallace's education it is hard to see him taking an active role in the proceedings. He would have lent weight and authority as a former Guardian, and certainly his passionate commitment to the Scottish cause must have made some impact. The Scottish envoys to Rome did achieve much, reflected in the increasingly dignified titles Balliol received in papal documents. In July 1299 he was mentioned as *called King of Scotland*; by November he was *King of Scots*; and by September 1300 he was *illustrious King of Scots.* In Scotland, too, Balliol's position was strengthened by Bruce's resignation from the Guardianship; his replacement was Sir Ingram de Umfraville, a kinsman of Balliol and a Comyn ally. Despite Balliol's increasing fortunes, however, Edward of England showed no sign of abandoning his attempts to dominate Scotland.

8–The Hammer of the Scots

Although baronial opposition had thwarted his attempt to
recapture Scotland in 1299, Edward did manage to mount a
campaign in the summer of 1300. The English still maintained a
grip on Lothian and the south-east; this time Edward would
campaign in the west. Assembling his army at Carlisle, he marched
north to Lochmaben Castle, which, although hard-pressed by the
Scots, remained in English hands. Relieving the garrison there, he
turned his attentions to the powerful Scottish-held Caerlaverock
Castle, an assault recorded in the 14th-century poem *Le*

Caerlaverock Castle – a fine moated castle, now ruinous.

Siège de Karlaverock written by a member of Edward's army.
Edward was by this time becoming increasingly frustrated and
angry with the continued resistance of the Scots, and the difficulty
he was having in stamping his will on his smaller, weaker
neighbour. He vented some of his rage on the Scots at
Caerlaverock, refusing them honourable surrender terms and,
after his siege engines had made short work of the fortifications,

hanging several members of the garrison for daring to resist him at all.

Edward then marched through Galloway to Kirkcudbright, where he met for a two-day parley with the Guardian John Comyn and his kinsman the Earl of Buchan. They demanded the restoration of King John, the recognition of Balliol's son Edward as heir to the Scottish throne, and the return of the English estates forfeited by the Scottish lords. If this was refused, they said, Scotland would continue to resist. It must have taken a great deal of courage to address so volatile a King as Edward I, at the head of a large army, in those terms. Edward, incandescent with fury, refused, and Comyn and the Earl of Buchan were probably lucky to return unscathed from the English camp.

Throughout July, August and September of 1300, Edward's army and the Scottish forces under Comyn, Umfraville and Lamberton manoeuvred against each other. Edward was desperate to get to grips with the Scots, but the Scots declined to oblige. Frustrated, with his barons increasingly keen to return to England, and having received Pope Boniface's demand for an Anglo-Scottish truce, this time addressed to him personally, Edward withdrew from Scotland in October 1300. He agreed to grant the Scots a temporary truce until 21 May 1301 and to release the Bishop of Glasgow, imprisoned in England since 1297. Scottish envoys met with Edward again in October, this time at Dumfries, and repeated their offer of peace. Edward laughed scornfully, declaring, *Each one of you has done homage to me as overlord of Scotland. Now you set aside your allegiance to me and mock me as though I were a weakling.* The Scots answered, *You should not laugh: we offer peace in all seriousness. Exert your strength and see if might will triumph over right or right over might.* Edward's answer was grim: *Take care that you do not come to me again.* Then he swore an oath that he would lay waste to Scotland from coast to coast and force the Scots to submit.

By early 1301, unable to agree, Comyn, Lamberton and

Umfraville all resigned as Guardians in favour of one man, Sir John Soulis. With a foot in both Comyn and Bruce camps, Soulis was seen as a neutral, a fervent supporter of an independent Scotland. Despite intense French and papal diplomatic pressure, Soulis faced Edward again in the summer of 1301. Again Edward brought a large army, this time including his son, Edward of Caernarvon, and recaptured several more castles in the south and west, but again he was unable to bring the Scots to battle. Although Edward wintered at Linlithgow, he was forced to make another treaty with the Scots, running from January to November 1302.

At the start of 1302, two very important events occurred. The first was news from the Continent: Balliol had been released by the Pope into French custody. Rumours began to circulate that he would shortly be restored to Scotland at the head of a large French army. It is about this time that William Wallace reappeared in Scotland, and it is possible that he brought this news himself. It is unclear whether these rumours had any substance to them, but they are certainly not inconceivable: Philip of France had become increasingly angry with Edward's continued assaults on Scotland. The second important event was directly linked to the first: Robert Bruce, Earl of Carrick – no longer a Guardian but still a powerful figure in the fight against the English – surrendered to Edward. Bruce feared that the return

Roslin Castle and Glen – see next page

of Balliol would result in the exaltation of the Comyn faction and the destruction of his family lands and power – not to mention the end to his hopes of becoming King of Scots. His surrender to Edward shows just how strong the rumours of Balliol's return must have been.

Bruce's defection was a major blow to the Scots, but worse still was to come. On 11 July 1302, in a startling echo of Stirling Bridge, the French chivalric host was trapped in a marsh at Courtrai by a rebellious Flemish peasant army and slaughtered. Philip IV's power was badly dented; whatever his plans had been, he was in no position to send a French army to fight in Scotland. Worse still, he became embroiled in a quarrel with the Pope which threatened to overshadow Scotland's cause.

In the autumn of 1302 the Scots sent a large and powerful delegation to Paris, which included John Soulis, Bishop Lamberton, Ingram de Umfraville, the Earl of Buchan, James Stewart and other notaries of Scotland: this was obviously a grave situation indeed. Back home, John Comyn of Badenoch resumed the post of Guardian, this time on his own.

The truce with Edward expired in November 1302, and once again William Wallace was at the forefront of Scottish resistance to English incursions. The English *Rishanger Chronicle* states that in 1303 the Scots began to attack English garrisons in Scotland, *making William Wallace their commander and captain*. On February 24 an English expedition into the Scottish-held lands west of Edinburgh was ambushed near Roslin; several English knights were killed or captured, and Edward's lieutenant in Scotland, Sir John Segrave, was badly wounded in the encounter. Although this was really only a skirmish, this and other Scottish assaults against English-held fortifications, led by Wallace, Comyn and Simon Fraser, prompted Edward to launch another full-scale invasion in the summer of 1303.

Despite all their efforts, the Scottish diplomatic mission to

France was a failure. In May 1303 the French and English signed a peace treaty from which the Scots were excluded, despite all the promises of Philip IV. Edward could now turn the full force of his military might against them. Despite stern Scottish resistance, Edward's march northwards was unstoppable, and by September he had penetrated all the way to Kinloss on the Moray Firth. Returning south, he made Dunfermline his winter headquarters.

Dunfermline Abbey – Edward stayed at the nearby Palace.

Scottish resistance continued, and Wallace played a prominent part in leading raids on English garrisons and supply lines. Belief in a final victory over Edward died hard. Bishop Lamberton wrote several letters to Wallace, exhorting him to do all he could to thwart the English and committing part of the revenues of his bishopric to Wallace's cause. But the Scots could not raise an army to match Edward's forces in the field; for all their valour, their luck had run out. In February 1304 a large body of English knights attacked and routed Wallace's small force at Happrew, a few miles west of Peebles, and by May Edward had settled down to besiege Stirling Castle, the last major fortification in Scottish hands. Edward's behaviour at Stirling shows how determined he was to crush Scottish resistance once and for all, and displays the viciousness to which many of the Plantaganet Kings of England were prone. Sir William Oliphant, captain of Stirling Castle, requested that he be allowed to send a message to Sir John Soulis in France asking for instructions either to surrender the castle or to defend it to the last. Edward refused this request, stating *If he thinks it will be better for him to defend the castle than yield it, he will see.* He spent the next three months bombarding the castle with every kind of siege engine he could lay his hands on. When the garrison asked if they could surrender with military honour, he again refused, threatening them with hanging and disembowelment. Even when the garrison offered to surrender unconditionally, Edward refused to accept until he had the chance to bombard the castle for a day with his latest siege engine, the *War-wolf*.

Edward's implacable hostility and the weakness of their position forced the Scots to surrender, and by the spring of 1304 all the Scottish leaders except Wallace, Fraser and Soulis had submitted to the English King. Edward was prepared to make a lasting peace, and although many of the prominent men of Scotland were fined or exiled for varying lengths of time the penalties imposed were not too severe. Edward was saving his vitriol for Wallace.

9–Treachery and Death

Edward's remorseless pursuit of Wallace is perhaps the greatest testimony to the problems he had caused the English and to his power as a symbol of Scottish resistance. Edward's orders have the character of a personal vendetta: *No words of peace are to be held out to William Wallace in any circumstances whatever unless he places himself utterly and absolutely in our will*; and *James Stewart, Sir John Soulis and Sir Ingram de Umfraville are not to have safe conducts nor come within the King's power until Sir William Wallace is given up*.

Fraser eventually submitted to Edward; John Soulis went into self-imposed exile in France, where he died some five years later. But there was to be no peace in Scotland under Edward until Wallace was given up. Edward made this very clear with a later command, equating loyalty to him with disloyalty to Wallace: *Sir John Comyn, Sir Alexander Lindsay, Sir David Graham and Sir Simon Fraser shall exert themselves until 20 days after Christmas to capture Sir William Wallace and hand him over to the King, who will watch to see how each of them conducts himself so that he can do most favour to whoever shall capture Wallace, with regard to exile or legal claims or expiation of past crimes*.

Wallace was now a fugitive in his own land. Although there were many in Scotland who would shelter him and help him, there were doubtless others who would give him up for reward or favour. For Wallace, the war with England never stopped, and he continued to resist as best he could. With a small band of followers he darted around Scotland, evading capture and harassing the occupying English forces.

The winter of 1304 turned to spring 1305; Edward I was by now an old man, worn out by war. In Scotland, it was rumoured that he was dying. Once again, as in 1296 and 1297, discontented men began gathering to Wallace, and there was a real chance that Scotland could once more throw off the English yoke. But it was not to be. A spy in the pay of Sir John Menteith, a Scottish knight, had joined Wallace's growing band of followers, and communicated his movements to his master. When Wallace was reported to be staying near Glasgow (modern-day Robroyston) in the house of one Robert Rae in July, Menteith struck. In the middle of the night, Menteith and his men burst in, overwhelming Wallace and giving him no chance of escape.

Wallace was dragged away and taken to Carlisle, where he was imprisoned and placed under the custody of Sir John Segrave. From Carlisle he was taken south, his hands roped behind his back and his legs tied together under the belly of his horse. The journey lasted 17 days, each day taking Scotland further away and bringing London and his arch-enemy closer. Wallace and his captors reached London on 22 August 1305, where he was brought before Edward. The English King, delighted that his enemy was at last in his grasp, ordered him to be taken to trial.

The next morning he was taken through the streets of London, past jeering crowds, to Westminster Hall. Inside the hall a scaffold had been built, on which Wallace was made to stand. A laurel wreath was placed on his head as an act of mockery and humiliation. Edward arrayed the full legal might of his realm against Wallace: Peter Mallory, chief Justiciar of England, was in charge of proceedings. This is not to say that there would be a trial in any modern sense of the word: Wallace was a condemned man before he set foot in Westminster Hall. But Edward I loved legal forms and practices, and wanted his show-trial to demonstrate that justice had been served.

No witnesses were called to this trial, there was no plea, and Wallace was given no opportunity to defend himself. The list of charges against him was impressive, including murder, arson, the destruction of property, and sacrilege: this referred largely to his raid on the north of England in 1298 and the burning of villages and churches. The one specific charge made against Wallace was the murder of William Heselrig, the English Sheriff of Lanark.

The Trial of Sir William Wallace

Wallace denied none of these accusations. He did, however, protest at the final charge: treason. Edward I was not his King, and

Wallace had never sworn allegiance to him. But here in London, Edward's word was literally law, and treason was whatever the King declared it to be.

From here there was only one possible outcome. Sentence was passed, condemning Wallace to the death of an outlaw and a traitor: hanging, drawing and quartering. Tied to a hurdle, Wallace was dragged along a circuitous route through the London streets to Smithfield Elms. There a noose was place around his neck and he was hoisted into the air. He was left swinging there, slowly choking, for five or ten minutes before being cut down again. Still alive – as was the plan – his abdomen was cut open and his entrails pulled out, to be burned on a bonfire in front of him. Then, and only then, was his head struck from his body by the blow of an axe and his body cut into four quarters.

Wallace's head was placed on a spike over London Bridge, and the four parts of his body were sent to Berwick, Perth, Stirling and Newcastle as a warning and a threat to any who would emulate him. Wallace was dead, the Scots crushed, and Scotland was amalgamated into a greater England: Edward's triumph was now complete.

But Edward would not enjoy his victory for long. Six months later, on 25 March 1306, Robert Bruce was crowned King of Scots and a new Scottish rebellion against English rule began. Edward, now 68 years old, was forced once again to march north with his army. He never reached Scotland. On 11 July 1307, Edward I died at Burgh-on-Sands on the southern shore of the Solway Firth, a few miles short of the Border. Although it took many more years of warfare, Scotland was to fight itself free from English rule.

In Edward I, Scotland had a remorseless and implacable enemy. But in William Wallace it had an indefatigable champion who refused to surrender. In the darkest days of 1296 and 1297 he had kept the flame of an independent Scotland burning; without his courage, determination and leadership, it is doubtful if the Scots would ever have won their freedom from the English. Even after Bruce's triumph at Bannockburn in 1314, and the eventual English recognition of Scottish independence in 1328, Scotland and England remained in a state of almost permanent warfare for hundreds of years, and in almost every encounter Scotland came off worst. And yet the name and deeds of William Wallace continued to inspire the people of Scotland to fight on, to have pride in their small land, and to resist the often overwhelming might of their powerful and aggressive southern neighbours.

Map 4: Places to Visit in Scotland

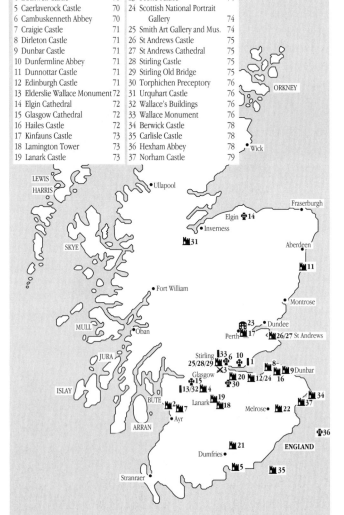

Places to Visit in Scotland

P	Parking
S	Sales Area
☕	Refreshments
wc	Toilet
£	Admission Charge
♿	Disabled
HS	Historic Scotland
NTS	National Trust for Scot.
EH	English Heritage

1 Alexander III Monument

NT 254864 66

On A921, E of Kinghorn, Fife

This monument, standing on King's Crag, marks the spot where Alexander III of Scotland fell to his death on the night of March 18, 1286.

Open all year

2 Ardrossan Castle

NS 233424 63

Off A78, in Ardrossan, Ayrshire

The ruins of a 15th-century keep stand on the site of an earlier castle, which according to some sources was captured by Wallace from the English. He slaughtered the garrison, heaping the bodies in the castle dungeon in an incident known as *Wallace's Larder*.

Open all year–ruin in a dangerous condition

3 Bannockburn Battlefield

NS 814917 57 NTS

Off M80/M9 at Junc 9, Bannockburn, 2 miles S of Stirling

Standing on the site of the battle of Bannockburn, the visitor centre also contains displays relating to William Wallace and Stirling Bridge. Nearby is the Rotunda and the famous equestrian statue of the King (opened

Ardrossan Castle

1964), situated where Bruce himself stood on the first day of the battle.

☎ 01786 812664—Battlefield open all year; heritage centre open March to 23 December

P S WC ℒ ♿ Facilities

4 Bothwell Castle

NS 688594 64 HS

Off B7071, 1 mile S of Uddingston, Lanarkshire

One of the finest early castles in Scotland. Of great strategic importance, it was besieged many times by all sides during the Wars of Independence.

☎ 01698 816894—Open all year except closed Thur PM and Fri in October to March

P S ℒ

5 Caerlaverock Castle

NY 026656 84 HS

Off B725, 7 miles SE of Dumfries, Dumfries

One of the finest castles anywhere in Scotland. In 1300, Edward I's 3000-strong army took two days to capture it from only 60 defenders, a deed commemorated in the medieval French poem *Le Siege de Karlaverok*.

☎ 01387 770244—Open all year

P S WC ℒ

6 Cambuskenneth Abbey

NS 809939 57 HS

Off A907, Cambuskenneth, 1 mile E of Stirling

Cambuskenneth Abbey, now ruinous, played an important part in the struggle for independence. Wallace's uncle was a priest at Dunipace, within the control of the Abbey, and it is likely that Wallace visited on several occasions.

View from exterior

Dirleton Castle – see next page

7 Craigie Castle

NS 408317 70

Off B730, 4 miles S of Kilmarnock, Ayrshire

This castle was the home of Sir William Wallace of Craigie, a 15th-century descendant of the elder brother of the Scottish hero. In the 1470s, Sir William commissioned Henry the Minstrel to write an epic poem commemorating the life of his famous ancestor.

View exterior

8 Dirleton Castle

NT 518840 66 HS

Off A198, Dirleton, 2 miles W of North Berwick, Lothian

Dirleton Castle fell to Edward's invading army in 1298 after a hard siege, shortly before the battle of Falkirk. It was eventually recaptured and partly demolished by the Scots in 1311. The castle was rebuilt, but is now a ruin.

Garden. Exhibition.

☎ 01620 850330—Open all year

P S ♿

9 Dunbar Castle

NT 678794 67

Off A1087, in Dunbar, East Lothian

Only the courtyard and foundations remain of a very ruined keep, from one of the strongest and most important castles in the south of Scotland. In 1296, a besieging English force destroyed a Scottish army sent to relieve the castle, bringing John Balliol's reign as King of Scots to an end.

Open all year –very ruinous

P Nearby

10 Dunfermline Abbey

NT 089873 65 HS

Off A907 or A823, in Dunfermline, Fife

Edward I stayed here on several occasions during his Scottish campaigns. After Iona, Dunfermline Abbey became the traditional burial place of the Scottish Kings. Bruce's tomb was rediscovered here in 1818 and is marked with a fine 19th-century brass. Ruins of the Royal Palace and domestic buildings lie next to the Abbey.

Exhibition.

☎ 01383 739026—Choir of church closed October to March

P Nearby S ♿

11 Dunnottar Castle

NO 882839 45

Off A92 or A957, 2 miles S of Stonehaven, Aberdeenshire

Built on a high promontory into the sea, Dunnottar is a spectacular and substantial ruin. A castle on this site may have been captured by William Wallace in 1296, and he reputedly had 4000 Englishmen burned to death here.

Steep climb to castle, and back.

☎ 01569 762173—Open all year except weekends in winter, 25–6 December & 1–2 January

P ♿

12 Edinburgh Castle

NT 252735 66 HS

Edinburgh

One of the greatest and most imposing castles in Scotland, which saw much action in the Wars of Independence. The Stone of Destiny is displayed in the castle along with the

Scottish Crown Jewels, as is the huge 15th-century cannon, Mons Meg. St Margaret's Chapel, dedicated to Queen Margaret, wife of Malcolm Canmore and built by her son David I, dates from the 12th century.

📞 0131 225 9846—Open all year; courtesy vehicle can take visitors with disabilities to Crown Square

🅿️ ☕ 🅂 ♿ ⛝ 🚾/Facilities

13 Elderslie Wallace Monument
NS 444632 63
On A737, Elderslie, Renfrewshire
Not to be confused with the larger and more famous National Wallace Monument in Stirling, this smaller memorial stands in the centre of Elderslie in Renfrewshire, the birthplace of Sir William Wallace.
  Stands on Johnstone Main Road.
📞 0141 889 0711
Open all year
🅿️ ♿ Access

14 Elgin Cathedral
NJ 222632 28 HS
Off A96, Elgin, Moray
Elgin Cathedral – once one of the finest churches in Scotland – is now in ruins. Edward I visited during his triumphant march around Scotland in 1296, and again in 1303. The nearby castle was retaken by the Scots in 1308 and destroyed. Exhibition.
📞 01343 547171—Open all year – joint entry ticket with Spynie Palace
🅿️ Nearby 🅂 ⛝

15 Glasgow Cathedral
NS 602655 64 HS
Centre of Glasgow
This Cathedral survived the Reformation intact and is still the Parish Church of Glasgow. Robert Wishart, Bishop of Glasgow, was a prominent supporter of Wallace and Scottish independence. Much of the building dates from his time (1271–1316).
📞 0141 552 6891—Open all year
☕ 🅂 🚾 ♿ Access

16 Hailes Castle
NT 575758 67 HS
Off A1, 1.5 miles W of East Linton
Substantial ruins of this very old and beautifully situated castle. Taken by the English in 1296, it quickly fell back into the hands of the Scots. Edward I recaptured it during his campaign of 1298, prior to the battle of Falkirk.
Open all year
🅿️

Hailes Castle

17 Kinfauns Castle

NO 151226   258

Off A85, 2.5 miles E of Perth

Site of a castle, of which nothing remains, on which a Gothic mansion was built in 1822. The castle was the property of the Charteris family, who are descended from Thomas de Longueville. Nicknamed *The Red Rover*, de Longueville was a French knight who turned to piracy. Wallace is supposed to have encountered him on his voyage to the Continent, captured him, and gained a pardon for him from Philip IV of France. De Longueville joined with Wallace, and fought for him. After Wallace's death de Longueville supported Bruce, who granted him the lands at Kinfauns in 1313.

View from exterior

18 Lamington Tower

NS 980320   72

Off A702, 5 miles SW of Biggar, Lanarkshire

The ruins of a 15th-century tower.

According to Henry the Minstrel, Marion Braidfoot, heiress to the Lamington estate, was betrothed to Wallace. She was killed by William Heselrig after she helped Wallace escape. In revenge, Wallace slew Heselrig, sparking off his campaign against the English.

View from exterior

19 Lanark Castle

NS875435   72

Off A73, in Lanark

The site of the castle where Wallace attacked and slew William Heselrig. Nothing remains, and its exact location is unknown.

20 Linlithgow Palace

NT 993774   65   HS

Off A803, in Linlithgow, West Lothian

This ruin, accidentally burnt by Government troops in 1746, stands on a mound overlooking Linlithgow Loch and has been much altered during its use. Edward I and his army camped

Gatehouse, Linlithgow Palace

here before marching to defeat Wallace's army at Falkirk.

☎ 01506 842896—Open all year

🅿 🆂 ♿

21 Lochmaben Castle

NY 088812 78 HS

Off B7020, 0.5 miles S of Lochmaben, Dumfriesshire

The ruins of a castle, which saw much action in the Wars of Independence.

Open all year – view from exterior

22 Roxburgh Castle

NT 713337 74

Off A699, 1 mile W of Kelso, Borders

Little remains of what was one of the most powerful castles in Scotland. Bishop Wishart was imprisoned in the castle in 1296, and Edward I marshalled his forces here before the battle of Falkirk.

Castle very ruinous

23 Scone Palace

NO 115267 58

Off A93, 2 miles N of Perth

The nearby Moot Hill was the ancient site of the inaugurations of the Kings of Scots. A replica of the Stone of Destiny, stolen by Edward I in 1296, is on display. Wallace attacked Scone in 1297 and drove the English justiciar, Ormesby, out of Scotland. Robert Bruce was crowned here in 1306.

 The present palace dates mostly from 1804 and is home to the Earls of Mansfield. Collections of furniture, clocks and porcelain. Gardens.

☎ 01738 552300—Open mid-April to October

🅿 ☕ 🆂 🆆🅲 ♿

♿ 🆆🅲/Facilities

24 Scottish National Portrait Gallery

NT 255743 66

Queen Street, Edinburgh

The Gallery possesses a large painting of the battle of Stirling Bridge by William Hole, along with a bronze cast of Robert the Bruce's skull. In September 1996 a reconstruction of Bruce's face was made using forensic techniques, and this forms part of a larger display on the Kings and Queens of Scotland. Also worth seeing is the mural of the Battle of Bannockburn.

☎ 0131 556 8921—Open all year except Christmas and New Year

🅿 Nearby ☕ 🆂 🆆🅲

♿ Facilities

25 Smith Art Gallery and Museum

Dumbarton Road, Stirling

Located in Stirling, this Art Gallery and Museum is presenting an exhibition on William Wallace until 15 December 1997. Titled *Scotland's Liberator*, this comprehensive exhibition illustrates Wallace's life and his effects on Scotland down to the present day. It also provides information on other notable Scots through the ages who are linked with William Wallace, and contains many unique items and displays.

☎ 01786 471917—Open until 15 December 1997

🅿 ☕ 🆂 🆆🅲

♿ Assisted access

Stirling Castle

26 St Andrews Castle

NO 513169 59 HS

Off A91, St Andrews, Fife

Close to the Cathedral, the castle of
the Bishops of St Andrews saw action
in the Wars of Independence

Visitor centre. Exhibition.

☎ 01334 477196—Open all year;
combined ticket available for castle
and cathedral

🅿 Nearby Ⓢ ⓦⓒ ♿ ♿ ⓦⓒ

27 St Andrews Cathedral

NO 516166 59 HS

Off A91, St Andrews, Fife

This cathedral was the centre for the
powerful and influential Bishop of St
Andrews. William Lamberton,
appointed Bishop on Wallace's
instructions in November 1297,
officiated here.

Museum houses a fine collection of
early Christian and medieval sculpture.

☎ 01334 472563—Open all year;
combined ticket available for
cathedral and castle

🅿 Nearby Ⓢ ♿

28 Stirling Castle

NS 790940 57 HS

Stirling

Stirling Castle, taken over by the
English in 1296, was recaptured by the
Scots following their victory at Stirling
Bridge, approximately one mile to the
north-east. Captured again by the
English in 1304 after a three-month
siege, Edward I refused to let the
defenders surrender until he had
tested his new siege-engine *War-Wolf*
on them for a day.

Visitor centre. Exhibition. Garden.

☎ 01786 450000—Open all year

🅿 ☕ Ⓢ ⓦⓒ ♿

♿ ⓦⓒ/Access

29 Stirling Old Bridge

NS 797945 57

Off A9, N of Stirling Castle, Stirling

Although this bridge was built in the
early 15th century, it stands only a
short distance from the site of
Wallace's crushing victory of 1297. The
road leading north from the bridge is
still called Causewayhead Road. Recent
archaeological investigations have

located what seem to be the original eight piers of the 13th-century structure, a few yards upstream of Stirling Old Bridge, running diagonally across the present-day course of the river.

Open all year

30 Torphichen Preceptory
NS 968725
Off B792, in Torphichen, West Lothian

An unusual and rather eerie place, Torphichen Preceptory was the main seat in Scotland of the Knights Hospitallers from the 13th century. William Wallace held a convention of Scottish nobles here in 1298, and Edward I was in residence after winning the Battle of Falkirk in the same year.

View from exterior

P Nearby

31 Urquhart Castle
NH 531286 26 HS
Off A82, 1.5 miles SE of Drumnadrochit, Highland

This castle was taken by the English in 1296, but Andrew Murray recaptured it in 1297 after ambushing the English constable, Sir William FitzWarin. He went on to retake several other northern castles, shortly before joining forces with Wallace prior to Stirling Bridge.

The fortress was dismantled in 1691 to prevent it being used by Jacobites. Impressive ruins remain.

☎ 01456 450551—Open all year

P **S** **WC** &

32 Wallace's Buildings
NS 442632 63
Off A737, in Elderslie, Renfrewshire

Reputedly on the site of William Wallace's birthplace in Elderslie, Renfrewshire, this 17th-century house was demolished in the 1970s, along with the farm of which it was part. All that remains are grassy mounds.

☎ 0141 889 0711—Open all year

33 Wallace Monument
NS 808956 57
Off B998, 1 mile NE of Stirling Castle

This famous monument to William Wallace stands on the Abbey Craig, where Wallace, Murray and their men positioned themselves before the battle of Stirling Bridge in 1297. An extensive display includes Wallace's huge two-handed broadsword. There is a steep climb (246 steps) up to the monument.

☎ 01786 472140—Open March to October daily; February & November weekends only

P **🍴** **S** **WC** &

& **WC**/Limited access

Wallace Monument

Places to Visit in England

34 Berwick Castle
NT 994535 75 EH
*Adjacent to Berwick Railway
Station, W of town centre*
Once the greatest trading port in
Scotland, Berwick changed hands
several times throughout the Wars of
Independence and was of extreme
strategic importance. Edward captured
the castle in 1296 and had the
inhabitants massacred. Now just inside
the English border, parts of the
Elizabethan fortifications still remain.

The castle, the ruins of which stand
near the station, is where the Ragman
Roll was signed in 1296.
Open all year

35 Carlisle Castle
NY 397563 85 EH
N of Carlisle town, Cumbria
An immense fortification in the north-
west of England. The scene of many

Anglo-Scottish confrontations
throughout its history, it was besieged
several times but never fell.

Wallace was held here on his way
south for trial in 1306.

☎ 01228 591922—Open all year
except Christmas and New Year

P Nearby S WC ₤

36 Hexham Abbey
*Off A69, 2 miles W of Hexham,
Northumberland*
Hexham Abbey is a beautiful and
ancient church which dates back to
Anglo-Saxon times, and is still used as
a parish church today. A favourite
target for Scottish forays across the
Border, it was visited by Wallace
during his raid on the northern
English counties in 1297. Wallace
issued the Abbey with a letter of
protection after some of his men stole

Norham Castle – see next page

the Abbey treasures. Advance notice is
required to gain access to the crypt.
☎ 01434 602031—Open all year
🅿 Nearby Ⓢ ♿ Lim access

37 Norham Castle
NT 907476 75 EH
*Off B6470, 6 miles SW of Berwick-
upon-Tweed*
A formidable English stronghold
almost exactly on the Scottish border.
Edward I held his court here in 1291
to decide the claims to the Scottish
throne, and here in 1327 the English
envoys awaited Bruce to start peace
negotiations. Between these two
events Norham suffered and withstood
many Scottish sieges and assaults.

  It was eventually destroyed in 1513
by James IV before the Battle of
Flodden.
☎ 0191 261 1585—Open all year
🅿 ☕ Ⓢ ᵂᶜ ♿
♿ ᵂᶜ/Access excl keep

The Legacy of William Wallace

William Wallace is without doubt Scotland's greatest hero. He is the supreme Scottish national icon, a symbol of freedom, of resistance to oppression and of the power of the common man. Although Robert Bruce led the cause of Scottish independence for 23 years, and finally forced the English to accept a separate Scotland, today the Scots see Wallace as the true hero. Yet in the records of his time he hardly figures at all.

The first Scottish chronicler to pay much attention to Wallace was *John of Fordun*. His chronicle was written in the latter half of the 14th century, and is the earliest surviving Scottish record to praise Wallace for his courage and patriotism. The huge epic poem *The Brus*, recounting the exploits of Robert the Bruce, written towards the end of the 14th century, does not mention Wallace at all. Probably the author, John Barbour, wished to skate over a period of history which did not reflect well on his protagonist's constancy to the Scottish cause.

To the upper ranks of Scottish society in the late 14th century, and especially to the Court, Robert Bruce was the real champion of Scotland and the heroic ancestor of the Stewart kings. These were the people whom poets and chroniclers wished to impress. It was not until around 1478, some 100 years after *The Brus* was written, that Henry the Minstrel wrote his poem praising Wallace. Henry, of course, was writing for his patron, Sir William Wallace of Craigie, a descendant of Sir Malcolm Wallace, the elder brother of the hero.

So does this mean that, in his time, Wallace was not the inspirational figure he has become today? Certainly Sir John Menteith, the Scot who betrayed Wallace to the English, was not at the time reviled in Scotland and indeed was one of the signatories of the Declaration of Arbroath, a stirring proclamation of Scottish independence sent by the Community of the Realm to the Pope in 1320. But the only records we have are those which survived the turbulent centuries to the present day; there may once have been a contemporary Scottish record of Wallace's exploits, and of course many more stories would have been in circulation which were never written down at all.

Robert Bruce and his followers did not resent Wallace, nor did they try to forget him and his deeds. But to them he was just not very important. He had, with Andrew Murray, led a Scottish army to a victory over the English; he had been made Guardian; he had been defeated by Edward and had resigned his Guardianship; and then he had more or less vanished from the historical limelight. As such he was no more or less remarkable than, say, Sir John Soulis. How was Wallace transformed into a national hero?

In truth, Wallace was a problem to the great men of his time. Unshakeable in his drive for Scotland's freedom, implacable in his hostility towards the English, he probably reflected the feelings of the lower end of Scottish society: the minor landed families, the peasants and the townspeople. Such emotions were very difficult for the nobility – with their cross-border ties of marriage, loyalty and land – to comprehend. They did not really see Scotland or England as separate units; each noble was lord of his own territory, and each had his own private army. They owed their monarchs military service as rent, but if they chose not to show up there was usually little the Scottish or English Kings could do to force them.

Even in defeat, the nobility generally did not suffer too much. Because they could be ransomed, they were more valuable alive than dead. It was also difficult, even for a powerful ruler, to force a noble family to surrender their lands. Usually, a victorious King would receive oaths of fealty from his defeated noble foes and – perhaps taking a hostage or two to ensure good behaviour – allow them to remain on their estates. Not for them the horrors of the sack of Berwick, or the slaughter at Dunbar or Falkirk. So it is easy to see that they might not have taken the Scottish defeat and subjugation of 1296 too seriously. They now paid homage to Edward instead of Balliol, but they still had their lands. They felt Edward's actions to be unjust, and were certainly not happy with the idea of fighting for him in France; but they also knew him to be getting old, so they were prepared to sign the Ragman Roll, and to wait and see what the future held.

The Scottish Church, however, was not. They were acutely aware of the Border, and of the threat to their power posed by English domination. Conscious of Scotland as a separate political entity, they were a major driving force behind the resistance to Edward. They would have preached the injustice of the English invasion, and the common people – who were suffering the most from the depredations of the English garrisons and officials – responded. They could see the invaders as different, and foreign; if their lords would not act to drive them out, then the commoners would.

This is why, today, Wallace is a hero. He was the captain of the first great national Scottish cause: the fight for freedom against the English. This struggle gradually built up a sense of unity, regardless of rank: rather than fighting for a lord or a King to whom they had personally pledged their faith, the Scots began to fight out of loyalty to an abstract idea of Scottish nationhood. Of course, this did not take place instantaneously or universally across Scotland: marriage, homage, blood, and self-interest remained the important factors for most individuals. But the concept was expressed, and it enlarged and strengthened the Community of the Realm.

By his words and by his deeds, and by his unswerving devotion to the Scottish cause, Wallace embodied the idea of Scotland as one nation and one people. Refusing to compromise or to surrender, he led the Scottish people and forced the Scottish nobles to fight for their freedom. Reflected in the mirror of Edward's hostility, the Scots began to see themselves as a separate entity, and the more the English attacked, the more determined the Scots became to resist them.

Most of Wallace's exploits, as told by Henry the Minstrel, are fictitious, but many of them contain at least a grain of truth. These had to come from somewhere. Henry claimed to have read an original account, written by Wallace's personal chaplain. Even if this biography did exist, there are no known copies today. But Henry could also have drawn on a wealth of oral history concerning Wallace, passed down among the families and communities who had fought beside the man himself. These folk stories and oral histories would have formed a major part of Scottish culture, both noble and common. Indeed, some of Henry's verses seem very similar in many respects to the tales of Robin Hood – a traditional Saxon story, possibly based on fact, which has now blended into myth.

But William Wallace is no myth. His actions and deeds, based on firm historical evidence, are heroic enough without the need for any embellishment: his fight against tyranny; his rise to prominence despite his lower social station; his continued resistance in the face of often overwhelming odds; and his refusal to abandon his cause. These characteristics, which many of his noble contemporaries would have seen as startling, confusing and inconvenient, have inspired later generations, in Scotland and across the world. True to his word, his land, and ultimately to himself, William Wallace remains one of the greatest and most remarkable figures of Scotland's past.

Index